BATCH BAKING

CYNTHIA BARCOMI

BATCH BAKING

CYNTHIA BARCOMI

Get-ahead Recipes for COOKIES,
CAKES, BREADS and MORE

CONTENTS

THE BATCH IS BACK

In the mid-twentieth century, food became cheaper and more accessible, and it stayed fresher longer. Consumers dispensed with the idea of regional harvesting and seasonal food. Somewhere in the world, someone was growing strawberries and you could have them!

The food industry developed packaged mixes and frozen meals, and showed us that we, too, could eat like astronauts. We no longer needed to squeeze oranges for their juice or peel potatoes, because we could *finally* re-constitute everything from a powder. This taught us we had more important things to do than stand in the kitchen. The food business modernized how we did things, made cooking easier, created less waste. It helped us to be more efficient in the kitchen… until it didn't. In fact, all these culinary shortcuts have led us to believe that we no longer have the ability or time to make things ourselves. Wrong. Enter Batch Baking. Homemade convenience.

What if we *like* standing in the kitchen cooking and baking? Does it make us happy? Does it make others happy? What role does great homemade food play in our quality of life?

You can make doughs, batters and lots more from scratch. You can store batches of batter in the fridge, pop some pre-shaped cookies in the freezer, and keep a sourdough starter going for years. Batch baking is efficient. No need to start from scratch every time you want to bake.

Enjoy the ride: the journey is the destination
These recipes are quick and easy. They are delicious and ready to go with simple prep. Go shopping and get inspired by what is in season. Taste, texture, shape, colour, smell – all these elements are a part of your journey in the kitchen. Enjoy the feeling of knowing exactly what goes into each dish and therefore what lands on your plate.

WHAT IS BATCH

Give it a rest

What happens to a dough made in advance? How long will it stay fresh? In general, doughs and batters benefit from a resting period in the fridge. This allows the gluten to relax and the dough to hydrate. For cookies and cake-ies this results in a more stable, even shape. Because of its complexity, a cookie dough is the most forgiving and can wait patiently in the fridge for up to 10 days! Keep doughs, batters, fillings and frostings fresh in airtight containers or wrapped airtight in cling film (plastic wrap).

Sleep

A sourdough starter can be a finicky thing for some people. Research has shown that using pineapple juice discourages the development of bad bacteria and encourages the growth of *the good guys*. Feed it, nurture it and the starter will be your friend.

No time to bake? Just set the sourdough starter in the fridge. It will nap peacefully until you need it. Take it out, feed it and in a matter of hours you will have an enthusiastic starter begging to become a batter, burger buns or pizza. If the starter has become tired and developed *hooch* (yes, alcohol), just pour it off or stir it in, feed it and it will come back to life!

Feel free to take your time baking once you've made something from the starter. A sourdough batter or dough can sleep for up to 5 days in the fridge, ready to go when you are. Think of the possibilities: a perfect pancake for breakfast, filled flatbreads for lunch and a yummy pizza for dinner. Easy.

Ovens

All my recipes are tested in a fan-assisted oven. If you are using a conventional oven, you may need to increase the cooking time slightly. I do not recommend increasing the temperature, simply get to know your oven and adjust the cooking time as needed.

BAKING?

Shape up and freeze right

The freezer is your friend. Sometimes you have more dough than you can use. Sometimes you need to plan ahead. Shaping and freezing most doughs is an option that buys you time and flexibility for those unexpected moments or cravings. Bake a cake, make the frosting, freeze them, forget them. The next time you're in a pinch, you've got a cake ready to come to life.

Not only can you freeze individual portions of cookie dough, but they will bake as quickly as fresh cookie dough. Freezing unbaked cake-ies in individual mounds affords you the luxury and flexibility of baking the amount you want when you want. Fresh and warm. Open freeze cookie dough or mounds of cake-ie batter on a plate. Once frozen, wrap airtight and pop back in the freezer.

Mix egg yolks with a big pinch of salt or sugar to prevent coagulation. Freeze the yolks individually in an ice cube tray. Simply thaw to use. Collect and freeze egg whites in a ziplock bag or an airtight container. Let them thaw in the fridge for a few hours and they are ready to go.

Freeze leftover frosting or buttercream for another day. Let it thaw on the counter or in the fridge, beat it again and achieve spreading perfection. Store anything you freeze airtight and mark it with name and date. Remember, you can only freeze and thaw something **once!**

Time is on your side

Yes, it is. A yeast dough benefits from a long, cold rise and can wait for up to 4 days in the fridge, all the while developing more flavour and texture. Refrigerating a yeast dough will reward you with flavour only attained through time and patience. If you need it sooner, simply let a portion of the dough rise on your counter for a couple of hours. Just don't rush it by putting it on top of your heater! And if you decide that time is of the essence, you can simply freeze the dough – either in a loaf pan or free-form. Let it thaw in the fridge overnight for a fresh loaf in the morning.

Extras

Garlic herb butter and slow-roasted tomatoes are two of my favourite savoury accompaniments. They make any bread even tastier.

When it comes to sweet accompaniments, be bold with frosting and buttercream flavours, but don't pile them on so thickly that you lose the balance between the vehicle and the topping. It's good to **want more** and disappointing to feel weighed down after enjoying a cake or pastry.

Enjoy life, enjoy food

At the end of the day, food is more than simply nourishment. It is a way of life, a culture, a philosophy. It brings people together. It's celebratory. If we are what we eat, then let's be the best we can be and bake the best we can bake. Together.

INGREDIENTS

Baking consists of several intertwined components: ingredients, instructions and equipment. Many people don't read through a recipe before starting it, which can be risky business, my friends. For this reason, I have tried to provide all the information you need about the ingredients within the ingredients lists, but have also compiled some essential knowledge here, which I recommend you read before embarking on the recipes.

When it comes to baking, nothing is easier or more precise than using a digital scale. Toss the cups and try it! Remember, the size of a baking pan is part of the recipe. Sure, you can use a different one, but you need to calculate the ingredients for that size to dispense with crossing your fingers! Success is a mathematical equation, not luck.

How much can you substitute in a recipe and still expect it to turn out right? Ingredients can be swapped out if you understand the role an ingredient plays in a recipe, and how combining ingredients affects them. There is a science to flavour and texture. For example, a ganache made with raspberry purée and dark (bittersweet) chocolate will be fruity and have a beautiful high note. If you substitute strawberries for the raspberries, you'll taste almost no fruitiness. Strawberries lack an assertive acidity and become overwhelmed in a ganache.

Here's my recommendation: I've done all the work to take the guessing game out of baking. Embrace the recipe! Surrender yourself and your kitchen – the recipe is your key to success.

Butter Always use unsalted butter and take note of its temperature in a recipe. Cold, softened or melted – these temperatures are part of your key to successful baking.

Chocolate Unless otherwise stated, I use bars of plain (semi-sweet) chocolate, melted or chopped. I love the texture of hand-chopped chocolate rather than chocolate chips.

PANTRY

Eggs It's almost impossible to buy a bad egg nowadays. A fresh egg will sink when placed in water; a bad egg will float. Eggs are easier to separate when chilled, but prefer to be room temperature when beaten to attain the most volume. When beating egg whites, wipe the inside of your bowl and all utensils generously with vinegar (or lemon juice) and salt. Not only does this ensure that everything is grease-free, it also stabilizes the beaten egg whites and prevents them from getting grainy.

Egg substitutes Depending upon the recipe, apple sauce, banana purée, linseeds (flaxseeds) and chickpea (gram) flour are all excellent plant-based binders.

Flour Most recipes use plain (all-purpose) flour, though some doughs benefit from the higher gluten content of strong bread flour. Substitute up to 25 per cent whole-grain flour in any given recipe. Remember, whole-grain flour contains less gluten, is heavier and absorbs more liquid than plain (all-purpose) flour. Take this into consideration when substituting.

Raising agents I use a few different types of raising agents in my recipes, and they all work slightly differently. These raising agents are not interchangeable.
- *Bicarbonate of soda (baking soda)* needs an acid (such as vinegar, lemon juice, yogurt, buttermilk or even molasses) to activate its leavening power.
- *Baking powder*, which is simply bicarbonate of soda (baking soda) plus potassium bitartrate (an acid), is double acting. It needs both liquid and heat to activate.
- *Instant dried yeast* is really convenient. It keeps forever and allows for the spontaneous baking of breads and flatbreads. No need to pre-activate it, simply mix it into your flour and make your dough.
- *Sourdough* is the leavening that needs the most time of any. Don't be afraid of making your own sourdough starter. Like a quirky friend, embrace it, care for it, love it. It is the gift that will keep on giving for years to come. See more detailed information on page 120.

Milk, buttermilk and plant-based milks Use whole milk; skimmed milk can be too watery. If you don't have buttermilk, use whole or skimmed milk plus a teaspoon of vinegar or lemon juice. For plant-based milk, I like to use pea protein or oat milk, always unsweetened. Nut milks are nice, but also bring their unique flavour to a recipe.

Nuts If you have the time, it's nice to toast nuts before using to bring out their flavour. If you toast them in a frying pan (no oil), set a timer for 7 minutes, keep an eye on them and flip them often. In the oven, simply set them on a parchment-lined baking sheet and toast in a 170°C fan (350°F/Gas 4) oven for 7 minutes until you can smell them and they're golden.

Salt I like to use fine sea salt in a recipe or flaky sea salt (such as Maldon) as a garnish. I love to bake with vanilla salt (see page 202). Coarse sea salt combined with finely grated lemon zest is a delicious garnish with a savoury dish or on a slice of bread with butter.

Cornflour (cornstarch) I often use cornflour (cornstarch) to lighten a cookie dough or cake batter. It lowers the gluten content and results in a lighter texture.

Sugar I love sugar! Sugar plays a multi-faceted role in baking, which makes it challenging to substitute. Not just sweet, sugar also supports and enhances the flavours of other ingredients. It binds, preserves and adds texture, colour and volume. Here are some of my favourite kinds:

- *White (granulated) sugar* is the standard sugar available in every supermarket. It is extremely refined, which is why it is so white. It doesn't have a lot of flavour, but does support the flavours of other ingredients. Use when you want a subtle sweetness, with no additional colour.
- *Caster (superfine) sugar* is a fine textured sugar. If you can't find it in your supermarket, simply finely grind regular granulated white sugar in a food processor. Use anytime you need sugar to dissolve fast, like when making meringues or certain buttercreams.
- *Brown sugar* is refined sugar with the molasses put back into it! You can make your own with a food processor: simply take 200g (1 cup) white granulated sugar, add 1–2 teaspoons black treacle (molasses) or dark golden syrup (corn syrup) and whip it up for a minute or two. It will not have the same depth of flavour as a true raw cane sugar, but is a good and thrifty alternative to impart a caramel flavour and add a bit of colour.
- *Icing (confectioners') sugar* is powdered refined sugar. Often a bit of cornflour (cornstarch) is added to prevent clumps from forming due to humidity. Do sift it; nothing is more disappointing than clumps of sugar in a frosting that should be completely smooth. You can try making your own icing (confectioners') sugar by grinding 200g (1 cup) white granulated sugar to a powder and adding 1 teaspoon cornflour (cornstarch). Use for glazes and quick frostings.
- *Raw sugars*, such as turbinado from Hawaii or Demerara from the Netherlands, often have rather large crystals and a faintly molasses flavour. They are produced directly from cane juice in sugar mills close to the cane fields. Use as a 1:1 substitute for refined sugar.
- *Unrefined sugars*, depending upon their origin, can be known as muscovado from Mauritius or the Philippines, panela from Colombia, or jaggery from India. These sugars are the least processed and retain much of their natural molasses. The cane juice is extracted, heated and cooled to form small, grainy crystals. Use in recipes where you can highlight their flavour and darker colour.

- *Simple syrup (liquid sweetener)* is an equal mixture of water and sugar, which is heated until the sugar dissolves. You can add flavours to it, such as schnapps, citrus zest or vanilla. Use to sweeten drinks or brush on the surface of a cake or cupcakes to keep them moist and add flavour.

Vanilla This is one of my favourite ingredients to use in baking. I like to make my own vanilla extract (see page 202) and enjoy using vanilla salt (see page 202), as well.

UTENSILS

What kitchen utensils do you *really need*? Any utensil is only as good as the person using it. Expensive kitchen gadgets alone aren't going to make you a successful baker, but a fantastic recipe coupled with some tried-and-true helpers will get you on your way. Be the best baker you can be and invest in solid products that will last (and skip the trendy stuff). Here's my advice.

Digital scales This is number 1 on my list. For precise, reliable baking, digital scales are much more accurate than measuring cups.

Stand mixer or hand-held electric whisk A stand mixer makes short work of cake batters and cookie doughs, and the dough hooks will knead a bread dough to perfection. Alternatively, use a hand-held electric whisk and a large mixing bowl.

Stainless steel mixing bowls These don't chip like glass bowls and aren't porous like plastic bowls. Foods cool quickly in metal bowls and the bowls will last a lifetime.

Wooden chopping (cutting) board Keep flavours separate by using one side for sweet ingredients and one side for savoury ingredients.

Baking pans I bake exclusively with anodized aluminium pans. They conduct heat quickly and evenly, can't rust, break or chip, and last a lifetime. It's useful to have the following: a 23cm (9in) square pan; loaf pans, big and small; a muffin pan; baking sheets; a 23cm (9in) pie or tart pan; and 15cm (6in) and 23cm (9in) round pans. Please avoid anything made of silicone; it doesn't conduct heat which is essential to baking.

Rolling pin I like the sturdy, streamlined, wooden French ones. They last a lifetime!

Rubber spatulas Big and small rubber spatulas are essential. I like to keep flavours separate, and have white ones for sweet foods and coloured ones for foods with onions or garlic.

Measuring spoons A set of measuring spoons will help you accurately measure out teaspoons and tablespoons.

Ice cream scoops Big and small ice cream scoops are useful for portioning out cookies and cake-ies.

Re-usable, airtight containers These are perfect for storing all your batches of batter, dough and frosting.

Bench scraper Important for dealing with soft doughs.

Cooling rack A wire rack allows air to circulate around your bakes while cooling.

Angled palette knives (metal spatulas) Big and small, these are useful for decorating those finished cakes and cake-ies.

Fine-mesh sieve (strainer) Necessary for sifting lump-free cocoa, spices and icing (confectioners') sugar.

Sharp knives Make the investment in some big and small sharp knives. It's worth it.

Four-sided grater Perfect for coarsely and finely grating cheese, and for zesting citrus fruits.

Whisks A big and a small hand whisk are invaluable for whipping things by hand.

Pizza cutter I use a pizza cutter for cutting rough puff pastry to size.

Timer Or simply use your phone. And definitely use it while you're roasting nuts!

Laser thermometer Found online and at any home improvement shop, a laser thermometer is inexpensive, easy to use and indispensable for making Swiss meringe buttercream (see page 210).

COO

KIES

COOKIES have been an important part of my life since I could speak – even before! I have used cookies to seduce, to bribe, to comfort and to get people off my back. Nothing offers instant gratification like a cookie. Before you dive into the delicious recipes, here are some general pointers to take on board. Trust me, you'll never buy supermarket cookies again.

PLEASE, FOR THE LOVE OF BUTTER, DO NOT OVERBAKE!

LET'S HEAR IT FOR THE DOUGH

An amazing cookie is the result of an amazing dough. First, lay out all ingredients at room temperature unless otherwise stated. This allows the dough to come together easily as each ingredient loves and cuddles with the next. Putting together cookie dough is like building a house. The foundation is butter or oil, sugar and, sometimes, eggs. Mix until you have a homogeneous, fluffy texture and take your time.

Which leads me to my next point: *please don't overwork the dough!* To make the best quality dough, go with the flow and do not stop and start. A cookie dough does not need to be kneaded like a yeast dough. In many recipes I have swapped out some flour for cornflour (cornstarch) to lower the gluten content. This makes a lighter, less cake-like cookie, with a texture I just love. I often prefer to stir the flour in by hand, to avoid overworking.

When it comes to shortbread dough, it's all about the texture. Use a portion of rice starch or oat flour for that slightly sandy texture – a good texture affects the flavour, and vice versa.

Bake

So now you've put together the ultimate cookie dough, please, for the love of butter, do not overbake! Baking a cookie is a bit like cooking fish – remove it from the heat just before it's done, because a cookie continues to cook and settle after you've taken it out of the oven. I know, I know... *how can you tell if a cookie is done?* Look at its colour, notice its smell. I often go to the oven right before the timer rings because I smell the 'doneness'.

In answer to the question 'how do I keep my cookies fresh?'... Honestly? Bake 'em and eat 'em. Nothing beats a hot cookie out of the oven. The beauty of batch baking means you can keep the dough in the fridge or freezer ready for fresh-out-of-the-oven deliciousness later in the week, month or year.

Chill

I love to keep a cookie dough in an airtight container in the fridge. Depending upon the dough, it will keep for up to 10 days or 2 weeks.

Freeze

Simply open freeze the dough in cookie portions (on a plate in the freezer), then wrap airtight and keep in the freezer for up to 6 months. When you're ready to indulge, just preheat the oven, pop them onto a baking sheet lined with parchment and bake as usual. The frozen cookies rarely take any longer to bake than those from the fridge. Don't ask me why!

CLASSIC CHOCOLATE CHIP COOKIES

I have been baking chocolate chip cookies *all my life*. For me, they are like a Band-Aid, a peace-pipe and an aphrodisiac all wrapped into one. This is my latest version of a classic.

MAKES 20

140g (1 cup) plain (all-purpose) flour

60g (scant ⅔ cup) cornflour (cornstarch)

½ tsp bicarbonate of soda (baking soda)

½ tsp baking powder

½ tsp vanilla salt (see page 202) or salt

250–300g (9–10½oz.) plain (semi-sweet) chocolate

125g (1 stick) butter, softened

90g (scant ⅔ cup) dark

brown muscovado sugar

90g (scant ½ cup) caster (granulated) sugar

1 egg

1 tsp vanilla extract (see page 202)

1. Mix the flour, cornflour (cornstarch), bicarbonate of soda (baking soda), baking powder and vanilla salt or salt in a bowl and set aside.
2. Coarsely chop the chocolate and set aside.
3. Using a stand mixer or hand-held electric whisk, cream the butter and sugars together until very light; this will take several minutes. Beat in the egg followed by the vanilla extract. Reduce speed to low, add the flour mixture and mix until just combined; 5–10 seconds. With a wooden spoon or spatula, mix in the chopped chocolate.
4. Transfer the dough to an airtight container and refrigerate for at least 30 minutes for the dough to hydrate before using.
5. When ready to bake, preheat the oven to 175°C fan (350°F/Gas 4) and line a baking sheet with parchment.
6. Using an ice cream scoop or a tablespoon, scoop out mounds of dough onto the lined baking sheet, leaving 5cm (2in) between them.
7. Bake in the preheated oven for about 11 minutes, or until golden. Let cool on the baking sheet for 10 minutes, then transfer the cookies to a wire rack to cool.

Chill
The dough can be kept in the fridge in an airtight container for up to 10 days.

Freeze
Shape the dough into mounds and open freeze. Once frozen, wrap airtight and freeze for up to 6 months.

Bake from frozen
Preheat the oven as above and bake on a lined baking sheet for about 11 minutes, or until golden.

VEGAN CHOCOLATE CHIP COOKIES

My husband is the 'great chocolate chip cookie taste-tester' and when I gave him one of these cookies, he went nuts. It just goes to show, you don't always need eggs and butter to bake a fantastic cookie!

MAKES 20

VEGAN

250g (1¾ cups) plain (all-purpose) flour

1 tsp baking powder

1 tsp bicarbonate of soda (baking soda)

1 tsp vanilla salt (see page 202) or salt

200g (7oz) vegan plain (semi-sweet) chocolate, coarsely chopped

75g (½ cup) raisins (optional, but delicious!)

120g (generous ½ cup) Demerara (raw) sugar

100g (⅔ cup) light muscovado sugar

125ml (½ cup) vegetable oil, such as canola or sunflower

60ml (¼ cup) water

2 tsp vanilla extract (see page 202)

1. In a large bowl, whisk together the flour, baking powder, bicarbonate of soda (baking soda) and vanilla salt or salt. Add the coarsely chopped chocolate and raisins (if using).

2. In another large bowl, beat the sugars with the oil, water and vanilla extract on high speed for 4 minutes or longer, until the mixture is thick and homogeneous. With a spatula or wooden spoon, mix in the flour, chocolate and raisin mixture.

3. Transfer the dough to an airtight container and refrigerate for at least 3 hours so the dough can hydrate and the gluten can relax.

4. When ready to bake, preheat the oven to 175°C fan (350°F/Gas 4) and line a baking sheet with parchment.

5. Using an ice cream scoop or a tablespoon, scoop out mounds of dough onto the lined baking sheet, leaving 5cm (2in) between them. Flatten them slightly before baking.

6. Bake in the preheated oven until golden, about 11–12 minutes. Let cool on the baking sheet for 10 minutes, then transfer to a wire rack to cool completely.

Chill
The dough can be kept in the fridge in an airtight container for up to 2 weeks.

Freeze
Shape the dough into mounds and open freeze. Once frozen, wrap airtight and freeze for up to 6 months.

Bake from frozen
Preheat the oven as above and bake the cookies on a lined baking sheet for about 11–12 minutes, or until golden.

COOKIES

OATMEAL COOKIES

For me, baking is often a type of sense-memory and these oatmeal cookies are no exception. Inspired by a recipe from my great-grandmother, Cora, I can still smell them in her kitchen. I love them because they are unlike any other kind of oatmeal cookie I've ever eaten. They are crisp and light with no eggs, raisins, nuts or chocolate. Pictured page 24.

MAKES 18

140g (1 cup) plain (all-purpose) flour

100g (1 cup) porridge oats

¼ tsp baking powder

pinch of salt

½ tsp bicarbonate of soda (baking soda)

1 tbsp hot water

125g (1 stick) butter, softened

100g (⅔ cup) light muscovado sugar

1 tsp vanilla extract (see page 202)

flaky sea salt/Maldon salt, for sprinkling

1. Combine the flour with the oats, baking powder and salt. Set aside.
2. In a small glass, dissolve the bicarbonate of soda (baking soda) in the hot water.
3. Using a stand mixer or hand-held electric whisk, beat the butter with the sugar. Add the vanilla extract and continue to beat until light and fluffy. Stir in the bicarbonate of soda (baking soda) water.
4. With a wooden spoon or a rubber spatula, mix in the dry ingredients just to combine.
5. When ready to bake, preheat the oven to 190°C fan (375°F/Gas 5) and line a baking sheet with parchment.
6. Drop dollops of dough from a teaspoon onto the baking sheet, leaving about 4cm (1½in) between them. With the heel of your hand, lightly flatten the cookies. Use the tines of a fork to make a criss-cross pattern on top of the cookies and sprinkle with a few flakes of sea salt.
7. Bake in the preheated oven for about 12 minutes, or until golden. Transfer to a wire rack to cool.

Chill
The dough can be kept in the fridge in an airtight container for up to 2 weeks.

Freeze
Shape the cookies on a plate and mark with the criss-cross pattern, then open freeze. Once frozen, wrap airtight and freeze for up to 6 months.

Bake from frozen
Preheat the oven as above, place the cookies on a lined baking sheet, sprinkle with sea salt and bake for 12 minutes, or until golden.

OATMEAL, WALNUT AND RAISIN COOKIES

What makes this recipe so special is the addition of freeze-dried berries. Their slight tartness and bright colour elevate a familiar, classic cookie to a modern delight! Pictured page 25.

MAKES 24

VEGAN

2 tbsp ground linseeds (flaxseeds)

80ml (⅓ cup) hot water

250g (1¾ cups) plain (all-purpose) flour

1 tsp bicarbonate of soda (baking soda)

½ tsp baking powder

1 tsp salt

½–1 tsp ground cinnamon

¼ tsp ground nutmeg

125g (1¼ cups) fine porridge oats

125g (1¼ cups) rolled (old-fashioned) oats

100g (⅔ cup) raisins

60g (½ cup) walnut or pecan halves, chopped

20g (¾ cup) freeze-dried berries (optional)

250g (1 cup plus 2 tbsp) vegan margarine, softened

125g (⅔ cup minus 2 tsp) caster (granulated) sugar

125g (¾ cup) light muscovado sugar

1 tsp vanilla extract (see page 202)

1. Mix the ground linseeds (flaxseeds) with the hot water and let sit for 10 minutes in the fridge until it becomes gelatinous.
2. In a large bowl, mix the flour, bicarbonate of soda (baking soda), baking powder, salt and spices. Set aside. In another bowl, combine the oats with the raisins, nuts and optional freeze-dried berries.
3. Using a stand mixer or a hand-held electric whisk, whip together the softened margarine and sugars until light and fluffy. Add the vanilla extract and linseed (flaxseed) mixture and beat for another 1–2 minutes until even lighter and fluffier.
4. Stir in the flour mixture, followed by the oat mixture. Do not overmix.
5. Transfer the cookie dough to an airtight container and refrigerate for 2 hours.
6. When ready to bake, preheat the oven to 175°C fan (350°F/Gas 4) and line a baking sheet with parchment.
7. Drop dollops of dough from a teaspoon onto the baking sheet, leaving about 4cm (1½in) between them. With the heel of your hand, lightly flatten the cookies.
8. Bake in the preheated oven for 10–12 minutes, or until golden. Let cool on the baking sheet for 5 minutes before transferring to a rack to cool completely.

Chill
The dough can be kept in the fridge in an airtight container for up to 10 days.

Freeze
Shape the dough into mounds, lightly flatten and open freeze. Once frozen, wrap airtight and freeze for up to 6 months.

Bake from frozen
Preheat the oven as above and bake on a lined baking sheet for about 11–12 minutes, or until golden.

COOKIES

OATMEAL COOKIES WITH CHOCOLATE AND DRIED CHERRIES

If you want to make a friend, give them a cookie. If you want to say you're sorry, say I love you, beg for anything... give them a cookie. This cookie.

MAKES 24

140g (1 cup) plain (all-purpose) flour

½ tsp bicarbonate of soda (baking soda)

½ tsp vanilla salt (see page 202) or salt

100g (1 cup) porridge oats

200g (7oz) plain (semi-sweet) chocolate, coarsely chopped

75g (½ cup) dried cherries, dried cranberries or raisins

50g (½ cup) flaked (sliced) almonds

140g (1 stick plus 1 tbsp) butter, softened

100g (½ cup) caster (granulated) sugar

100g (scant ⅔ cup) light soft brown sugar

1 egg

1 tsp vanilla extract (see page 202)

1. In a medium bowl combine the flour, bicarbonate of soda (baking soda), vanilla salt or salt, oats, chocolate, dried cherries, dried cranberries or raisins, and flaked (sliced) almonds. Set aside.

2. Using a stand mixer or electric hand-held whisk, beat the butter and sugars until creamy. Beat in the egg and vanilla extract. Mix in the dry ingredients just until combined. Do not overmix the dough.

3. When ready to bake, preheat the oven to 175°C fan (350°F/Gas 4) and line a baking sheet with parchment.

4. Using an ice cream scoop or a tablespoon, scoop out mounds of dough onto the lined baking sheet, leaving about 4cm (1½in) between them. Lightly flatten the cookies.

5. Bake in the preheated oven for 12 minutes, or until golden. Allow to cool on the baking sheet; they firm up as they cool.

Chill
The dough can be kept in an airtight container in the fridge for up to 10 days.

Freeze
Shape the dough into mounds and open freeze. Once frozen, wrap airtight and freeze for up to 6 months.

Bake from frozen
Preheat the oven as above and bake the cookies on a lined baking sheet for about 12–13 minutes, or until golden.

PEANUT BUTTER MISO COOKIES

These peanut butter cookies with miso are out of this world. And… they are made without flour, so they're gluten free! The miso acts as a flavour enhancer and gives these innocent little cookies a real depth of flavour. Do use a light miso; the darker one tends to overpower the nuttiness of the flavour.

MAKES 18

GLUTEN-FREE

100g (⅔ cup) light or dark muscovado sugar

100g (½ cup) caster (granulated) sugar

1 tsp bicarbonate of soda (baking soda)

½ tsp baking powder

¾ tsp vanilla salt (see page 202) or salt

250g (1¼ cups) smooth peanut butter

1 egg

40g (2¾ tbsp) light miso

1. In a large bowl, whisk together the sugars, bicarbonate of soda (baking soda), baking powder and vanilla salt or salt.
2. Using a stand mixer or hand-held electric whisk, beat together the peanut butter and sugar mixture until fluffy. Add the egg and light miso. Continue to beat for about 30 seconds.
3. When ready to bake, preheat the oven to 180°C fan (350°F/Gas 4) and line a baking sheet with parchment.
4. Using an ice cream scoop or a tablespoon, scoop out mounds of dough onto the lined baking sheet, leaving about 4cm (1½in) between the cookies.
5. Bake in the preheated oven for 10–11 minutes, or until golden. Allow to cool on the baking sheet for 10 minutes before carefully transferring to a wire rack to cool completely.

Chill
The dough can be kept in the fridge in an airtight container for up to 10 days.

Freeze
Shape the dough into mounds and open freeze. Once frozen, wrap airtight and freeze for up to 6 months.

Bake from frozen
Preheat the oven as above and bake the cookies on a lined baking sheet for about 10–11 minutes, or until golden.

TAHINI COOKIES SPRINKLED WITH RAW SUGAR AND SESAME SEEDS

I admit it. I am powerless over these cookies. Regardless of *what* you do, they bake up perfectly round! Then there's the sweet and salty, winey-miso-sesame flavour. Perfect!

MAKES 16-20

VEGAN

1 tbsp finely ground linseeds (flaxseeds)

3 tbsp hot water

150g (1 cup plus 2 tbsp) plain (all-purpose) flour

½ tsp baking powder

1 tsp bicarbonate of soda (baking soda)

½ tsp vanilla salt (see page 202) or salt

200g (¾ cup plus 2 tbsp) tahini, well stirred

50g (3½ tbsp) light miso

120g (generous ½ cup) Demerara (raw) sugar

120g (¾ cup) light muscovado sugar

4 tbsp water

1 tbsp vanilla extract (see page 202)

For dredging

20g (2½ tbsp) sesame seeds

20g (1½ tbsp) Demerara (raw) sugar

1. Begin by mixing the ground linseeds (flaxseeds) with the hot water. Let sit for about 10 minutes in the fridge until it becomes gelatinous.
2. Mix the flour, baking powder, bicarbonate of soda (baking soda) and vanilla salt or salt in a large bowl. Set aside.
3. Using a stand mixer or hand-held electric whisk, whip up the tahini, miso and sugars (the mixture is quite thick). Stir in the water, followed by the vanilla extract and linseed (flaxseed) mixture. Add the flour mixture. Stir just until it comes together.
4. Transfer the dough to an airtight container and refrigerate for at least 2 hours.
5. When ready to bake, preheat the oven to 180°C fan (350°F/Gas 4) and line a baking sheet with parchment.
6. Combine the sesame seeds and sugar for dredging. With a tablespoon, dredge small balls of dough into the sesame/sugar mixture. Place on the lined baking sheet 4cm (1½in) apart and, with the heel of your hand, flatten them slightly.
7. Bake in the preheated oven for 11–12 minutes, or until golden. Let cool on the baking sheet for 10 minutes, then transfer to a wire rack to cool completely.

Chill

The dough can be stored in an airtight container in the fridge for up to 2 weeks.

Freeze

Shape the dough into mounds and open freeze. Once frozen, wrap airtight and freeze for up to 6 months.

Bake from frozen

Preheat the oven as above and bake the cookies on a lined baking sheet for about 11–12 minutes, or until golden.

CHEWY BROWN SUGAR GINGER COOKIES

What I appreciate most about these cookies: they are not Christmassy. Make them all year round and make sure not to overbake them. Keep them soft and chewy – my dream!

MAKES 24

300g (2¼ cups) plain (all-purpose) flour

1½ tsp bicarbonate of soda (baking soda)

½ tsp baking powder

½ tsp salt

1 tsp ground cinnamon

1½ tsp ground ginger

pinch of ground cloves

175g (1½ sticks) butter, softened

175g (scant 1¼ cups) dark brown muscovado sugar or dark soft brown sugar

1 egg

100g (5 tbsp) black treacle/molasses (or use golden syrup/light corn syrup for a lighter flavour)

For dredging

50g (scant ¼ cup) caster (superfine) sugar

1 tsp ground ginger and/or ground cinnamon

1. In a large bowl, whisk together the flour with the bicarbonate of soda (baking soda), baking powder, salt and spices. Set aside.
2. Using a stand mixer or hand-held electric whisk, beat the butter and sugar until light and creamy. Add the egg and beat until fluffy. Add the black treacle and mix until well combined. On low speed, or simply by hand, mix in the flour mixture until well combined. Do not overmix.
3. Transfer the dough to an airtight container and refrigerate for 2 hours.
4. When ready to bake, preheat the oven to 175°C fan (350°F/Gas 4) and line a baking sheet with parchment. Mix the sugar and spice(s) for dredging.
5. Using an ice cream scoop or tablespoon, scoop out balls of dough and dredge in the sugar and spice(s). Place on the lined baking sheet, 5cm (2in) apart.
6. Bake in the preheated oven for 10–12 minutes, or until golden, then transfer to a wire rack to cool.

Chill
The dough can be kept in the fridge in an airtight container for up to 10 days.

Freeze
Shape the dough into mounds and open freeze (without dredging in the sugar and spices). Once frozen, wrap airtight and freeze for up to 6 months.

Bake from frozen
Preheat the oven as above. Dredge the cookies in the sugar and spice(s) and bake on a lined baking sheet for 10–12 minutes, or until golden.

DOUBLE CHOCOLATE CHIP COOKIES

Usually I am quite the chocolate-purist when it comes to double choc chip cookies, but I simply could not resist including an option of adding chunks of walnuts to this vegan dough. I love the colour contrast and am partial to California walnuts for their buttery flavour. Pecans would work well, too.

MAKES 20

VEGAN

200g (scant 1½ cups) plain (all-purpose) flour

50g (½ cup) unsweetened cocoa powder

1 tsp baking powder

½ tsp bicarbonate of soda (baking soda)

¾ tsp vanilla salt (see page 202) or salt

1 tsp instant espresso powder (optional)

300g (10½oz) vegan plain (semi-sweet) chocolate, roughly chopped

125g (scant ⅔ cup) Demerara (raw) sugar

125g (¾ cup) light or dark brown muscovado sugar

125ml (½ cup) vegetable oil

1 tbsp vanilla extract (see page 202)

80ml (⅓ cup) water

75g (scant ⅔ cup) walnut halves, barely broken up (optional, but delicious!)

1. In a large bowl, whisk together the flour, cocoa, baking powder, bicarbonate of soda (baking soda), vanilla salt or salt and espresso powder, if using. Add the chopped chocolate. Set aside.

2. In another large bowl, beat the sugars with the oil, vanilla extract and water on high speed for 4 minutes until the mixture is thick and homogeneous. With a spatula or wooden spoon, mix in the flour mixture, and the walnuts, if using.

3. Transfer the dough to an airtight container and refrigerate for at least 3 hours so the dough can hydrate and the gluten can relax.

4. When ready to bake, preheat the oven to 175°C fan (350°F/Gas 4) and line a baking sheet with parchment.

5. Using a tablespoon, ice cream scoop or simply your hand, scoop out mounds of dough onto the lined baking sheet, leaving 5cm (2in) between them. No need to flatten them before baking.

6. Bake in the preheated oven for 11–12 minutes. Let the cookies rest on the baking sheet for 10 minutes before transferring to a wire rack to cool completely.

Chill
The dough can be kept in the fridge in an airtight container for up to 2 weeks.

Freeze
Shape the dough into mounds and open freeze. Once frozen, wrap airtight and freeze for up to 6 months.

Bake from frozen
Preheat the oven as above and bake the cookies on a lined baking sheet for 11–12 minutes.

TURMERIC GINGER SNICKERDOODLES

These snickerdoodles are the epitome of a modern classic. My great grandmother used to bake them in the late 1800s, followed by generations of bakers in my family. It is I who has decided to give a little makeover, inspired by the *golden milk* trend. Enjoy!

MAKES 24

325g (2⅓ cups) plain (all-purpose) flour

1 tsp baking powder

1 tsp bicarbonate of soda (baking soda)

1 tsp vanilla salt (see page 202) or salt

250g (2 sticks) butter, softened

275g (1⅓ cups plus 1 tbsp) caster (granulated) sugar

1 tsp ground turmeric

1 tsp ground ginger

2 eggs

1 tsp vanilla extract (see page 202)

For dredging

100g (scant ½ cup) caster (superfine) sugar

1 tsp ground ginger

1 tsp ground turmeric

½ tsp ground cinnamon (optional)

1. In a small bowl, whisk together the flour, baking powder, bicarbonate of soda (baking soda) and vanilla salt or salt. Set aside.
2. Using a stand mixer or electric hand-held whisk, beat together the softened butter and sugar until creamy. Add the turmeric, ginger and eggs, and beat for 3 minutes until light and fluffy. Beat in the vanilla extract. Add the flour mixture on low speed or stir it in with a wooden spoon, being careful not to overmix.
3. Place the cookie dough in an airtight container. Refrigerate for at least 1 hour.
4. When ready to bake, preheat the oven to 190°C fan (375°F/Gas 5) and line a baking sheet with parchment. Mix together the ingredients for dredging.
5. Using an ice cream scoop, a tablespoon or your hands, shape the dough into rounds about the size of a golf ball, dredge in the spiced sugar and place onto the lined baking sheet about 6cm (2¼in) apart. No need to flatten!
6. Depending upon the size, bake for 10–13 minutes. Let cool on the baking sheet for 5 minutes before transferring them to a rack to cool completely.

Chill
The dough can be stored in an airtight container in the fridge for up to 10 days.

Freeze
Shape the dough into mounds and open freeze without dredging in the sugar and spice(s). Once frozen, wrap airtight and freeze for up to 6 months.

Bake from frozen
Preheat the oven as above. Dredge the cookies in the sugar and spice(s) and bake on a lined baking sheet for 10–13 minutes.

COOKIES

BLONDIE COOKIES

I love brownies, and am a big fan of blondies, as well. They're often a bit of an *underdog* to a brownie's intense chocolate flavour and gooey texture. Not anymore. Enjoy this browned-butter version of a classic!

MAKES 20

180g (1½ sticks) butter, cut into chunks

180g (1⅓ cups) plain (all-purpose) flour

40g (scant ½ cup) cornflour (cornstarch)

1 tsp baking powder

½ tsp vanilla salt (see page 202) or salt

100g (½ cup) caster (granulated) sugar or Demerara (raw) sugar

80g (½ cup) light soft brown sugar

1 tbsp vanilla extract (see page 202)

1 egg, cold

sea salt flakes, to decorate

1. First, brown the butter. Melt the butter in a pan, preferably with a light-coloured base so you can see the colour of the butter as it browns. Once melted, boil for 4–4½ minutes, occasionally swirling the pan, until the butter is light brown. Do not let it burn. Water evaporates and the milk solids separate to caramelize, which gives the butter a nutty flavour and darker colour! Pour the browned butter into a large bowl to stop the browning. Set aside to cool for a few minutes.
2. In another large bowl, combine the flour, cornflour (cornstarch), baking powder and vanilla salt or salt. Set aside.
3. Using a stand mixer or hand-held electric whisk, beat the sugars into the butter, followed by the vanilla extract. Add the egg and beat until the mixture is thick and homogeneous. With the mixer on low speed, or using a rubber spatula, stir in the flour mixture.
4. Transfer the dough to an airtight container and refrigerate for 1 hour.
5. When ready to bake, preheat the oven to 175°C fan (350°F/Gas 4) and line a baking sheet with parchment.
6. Using an ice cream scoop or a tablespoon (the dough will be rather stiff now), scoop out mounds of dough onto the baking sheet, leaving 5cm (2in) between them. No need to flatten them!
7. Bake in the preheated oven for about 11 minutes, or until golden.
8. Transfer the cookies to a wire rack and immediately sprinkle with sea salt flakes.

Chill
The dough can be kept in the fridge in an airtight container for up to 10 days.

Freeze
Shape the dough into mounds and open freeze. Once frozen, wrap airtight and freeze for up to 6 months.

Bake from frozen
Preheat the oven as above and bake the cookies on a lined baking sheet for about 11 minutes, or until golden.

TAHINI SESAME SLICE-AND-BAKE COOKIES

I love baking with tahini! It can seamlessly morph from savoury to sweet, as in this recipe. A tasty cross between a slice of halva and a cookie – that's a global hybrid.

MAKES 24

225g (1⅔ cups) plain (all-purpose) flour

¼ tsp vanilla salt (see page 202) or salt

125g (scant ⅔ cup) Demerara (raw) sugar

125g (1 stick) butter, softened

100g (scant ½ cup) tahini

50g (2 tbsp) honey

1 tsp vanilla extract (see page 202)

For rolling

20g (3 tbsp) pistachios, chopped

10g (1 tbsp) sesame seeds

1. In a large bowl, whisk together the flour and vanilla salt or salt.
2. With a stand mixer or hand-held electric whisk, beat the sugar and butter until fluffy. Add the tahini, honey and vanilla extract, and beat until well combined. Slowly add the flour and salt. Mix only enough to thoroughly combine. Do not overmix. The dough might seem a bit soft, but this is correct.
3. Have a large piece of parchment ready. Turn the dough directly onto the parchment. Shape into a log about 6cm (2¼in) in diameter. Put the chopped pistachios and sesame seeds onto the parchment next to the dough and roll the dough over them to coat the outside in the nuts and seeds. Wrap tightly in the parchment, making sure that the ends are completely covered.
4. Chill the dough for at least 2 hours.
5. When ready to bake, preheat the oven to 175°C fan (350°F/Gas 4) and line a baking sheet with parchment.
6. Remove the dough from the fridge and, with a sharp knife, cut into 5mm (¼in) thick rounds and place on the baking sheet.
7. Bake in the preheated oven for about 12 minutes, or until golden. Let cool on the baking sheet for 10 minutes, then transfer to a wire rack to cool completely.

Chill

The dough can be kept in the fridge, wrapped airtight, for up to 2 weeks.

Freeze

The dough can either be frozen as a log or as sliced rounds for up to 6 months. Simply wrap airtight and freeze.

Bake from frozen

Preheat the oven as above and bake cookie slices on a lined baking sheet for 12–13 minutes. To bake from a frozen log, let the dough thaw enough to slice and bake as above.

TRIPLE NUT SHORTIES

These cookies have always been a favourite of mine and I used to love watching my grandmother bake them. I have taken the liberty of adding walnuts and almonds.

MAKES 30

75g (⅔ cup) pecan halves

75g (scant ⅔ cup) walnut halves

75g (scant ⅔ cup) pistachios or 75g (scant 1 cup) flaked (sliced) almonds

300g (2¼ cups) plain (all-purpose) flour

1 tsp baking powder

1 tsp bicarbonate of soda (baking soda)

½ tsp vanilla salt (see page 202) or salt

250g (2 sticks) butter, softened

125g (¾ cup) light muscovado sugar

125g (⅔ cup minus 2 tsp) caster (granulated) sugar

1 egg

1 tsp vanilla extract (see page 202)

1. Begin by toasting the nuts. Preheat the oven to 175°C fan (350°F/Gas 4) and line a baking sheet with parchment. Spread the nuts on the parchment. Bake for 7–9 minutes until you can smell their toasted aroma. Simply lift the parchment off the baking sheet to let the nuts cool. When cooled, chop them finely enough so it's easy to cut the dough, but not so finely that they turn into dust!

2. In a large bowl, combine the flour, baking powder, bicarbonate of soda (baking soda) and vanilla salt or salt. Add the cooled, chopped nuts. Set aside.

3. With a stand mixer or hand-held electric whisk, beat the butter with the sugars for several minutes until fluffy. Beat in the egg and the vanilla extract. On slow speed, add the flour mixture and mix enough to combine. Do not overmix.

4. For ease, divide the dough in half. Shape each half into a log, about 6cm (2¼in) in diameter and wrap in parchment. Refrigerate for at least 6 hours.

5. When ready to bake, preheat the oven to 175°C fan (350°F/Gas 4) and line a baking sheet with parchment.

6. Remove the dough from the fridge and, with a very sharp knife, slice off rounds about 6mm (¼in) thick. Place about 5cm (2in) apart on the lined baking sheet.

7. Bake in the preheated oven for 10–12 minutes, or until golden. Let cool on the sheet for 10 minutes before transferring to a wire rack to cool completely.

Chill
The dough can be kept in the fridge, wrapped airtight, for up to 10 days.

Freeze
The dough can either be frozen as a log or as sliced rounds for up to 6 months. Simply wrap airtight and freeze.

Bake from frozen
Preheat the oven as above and bake cookie slices on a lined baking sheet for 10–12 minutes. To bake from a frozen log, let the dough thaw enough to slice and bake as above.

SLICE-AND-BAKE CLASSIC SAND TARTS

I wanted to develop a cookie *less plain* than a simple sugar cookie. These sand tarts hit the mark. They remind me of childhood breakfasts of cereal with fresh strawberries.

MAKES 48

385g (2¾ cups) plain (all-purpose) flour

¾ tsp vanilla salt (see page 202) or salt

1 tsp baking powder

50g (1½ cups loosely packed) freeze-dried strawberries or freeze-dried mixed berries, finely ground

250g (2 sticks) butter, softened

225g (1 cup plus 2 tbsp) caster (granulated) sugar

1 egg

1. Combine the flour with the vanilla salt or salt, baking powder and ground freeze-dried berries. Set aside.
2. With a stand mixer or hand-held electric whisk, beat the butter and sugar until light and fluffy; about 2 minutes. Add the egg and beat for 2 minutes.
3. Stir in the flour mixture by hand, using a rubber spatula or a wooden spoon until it is incorporated. Be mindful not to overmix.
4. Shape the dough into a log, about 5–9cm (2–3½in) wide, wrap in parchment and set in the fridge to chill for at least 4 hours.
5. When ready to bake, preheat the oven to 175°C fan (350°F/Gas 4) and line a baking sheet with parchment.
6. Remove the dough from the fridge and, with a sharp knife, cut into 5mm (¼in) thick rounds and place on the baking sheet.
7. Bake in the preheated oven for around 11 minutes. Don't overbake and don't let the cookies take on too much colour. Let cool on the baking sheet for 5 minutes before transferring to a rack to cool completely.

Tip You can also roll out the dough to about 5mm (¼in) thick and cut out cookies using a cookie cutter.

Chill
The dough can be kept in the fridge, wrapped airtight for 10 days.

Freeze
The dough can either be frozen as a log or as sliced rounds for up to 6 months. Simply wrap airtight and freeze.

Bake from frozen
Preheat the oven as above and bake cookie slices on a lined baking sheet for 11 minutes. To bake from a frozen log, let the dough thaw enough to slice and bake as above.

SAND TART COOKIE SANDWICHES

Slice-and-bake Sand Tarts are delicious when paired up and sandwiching an indulgent ganache filling. I use a fruit ganache here, but they can also be filled with Cream Cheese Frosting (see page 206) for a creamy taste. Pictured page 49.

MAKES 24

250g (8½oz) fresh or frozen raspberries

300g (10½oz) plain (semi-sweet) chocolate, finely chopped

200ml (¾ cup plus 1½ tbsp) double (heavy) cream

1 x quantity Slice-and-bake Classic Sand Tarts (see page 44)

1. Start by making the raspberry purée for the ganache filling. Put the raspberries in a pan and heat gently until softened. Press the raspberries through a fine mesh sieve (strainer) and discard the seeds. You should have about 100ml (scant ½ cup) raspberry purée.
2. To make the ganache, place the chocolate in a large bowl and set aside.
3. Heat the cream and raspberry purée in a small pan until the mixture reaches boiling point. Pour it over the chocolate. Cover, without stirring, and leave for 5 minutes.
4. Uncover and stir with a whisk until the chocolate is completely melted and the mixture is smooth. Cool the ganache to room temperature, then refrigerate until it is a thick spreading consistency; about 2 hours.
5. Take one cookie and spread a little ganache over the flat side. Top with a second cookie and gently press them together. Repeat with the remaining cookies and ganache.

GRAHAM CRACKER SLICE-AND-BAKE COOKIES

I haven't missed much since moving to Europe, but oh how I missed graham crackers. As a child I ate them in the back of the car on the way home from dance class, ground them up to make a base (crust) for cheesecake, and made s'mores by the camp fire.

MAKES 30

200g (scant 1½ cups) plain (all-purpose) flour

125g (scant 1 cup) whole-wheat flour

30g (generous ¼ cup) wheatgerm

½ tsp vanilla salt (see page 202) or salt

½ tsp ground cinnamon

½ tsp bicarbonate of soda (baking soda)

½ tsp baking powder

250g (2 sticks) butter, softened

90g (scant ½ cup) brown sugar

2 tbsp runny honey

1 tbsp vanilla extract (see page 202)

For topping

1 tsp ground cinnamon

2 tbsp caster (granulated) sugar

1. In a large bowl, whisk together the flours, wheatgerm, vanilla salt or salt, cinnamon, bicarbonate of soda (baking soda) and baking powder. Set aside.
2. Using a stand mixer or hand-held electric whisk, beat the butter with sugar and honey until fluffy. Add the vanilla extract and continue to beat. Slowly add the flour mixture and mix only enough to thoroughly combine. Do not overmix.
3. Place the dough onto a big piece of parchment. Shape into a 5cm (2in) diameter log and wrap airtight. Chill for at least 4 hours.
4. When ready to bake, preheat the oven to 180°C fan (350°F/Gas 4) and line a baking sheet with parchment. Combine the cinnamon with the sugar for topping.
5. Remove the dough from the fridge and, with a very sharp knife, slice off rounds about 5mm (¼in) thick. Place on the lined baking sheet 5cm (2in) apart and prick each cookie several times with a fork. Sprinkle with cinnamon and sugar.
6. Bake in the preheated oven for 12–13 minutes, or until dark golden. Let cool on the baking sheet for 10 minutes before transferring to a rack to cool completely.

Chill
The dough can be kept wrapped airtight in the fridge for up to 2 weeks.

Freeze
The dough can either be frozen as a log or as sliced cookies for up to 6 months. Simply wrap airtight and freeze.

Bake from frozen
Preheat the oven as above and bake cookie slices on a lined baking sheet for 12–13 minutes. To bake from a frozen log, let the dough thaw enough to slice and bake as above.

S'MORES

Though I feel like a real city girl, I used to love sitting around a campfire toasting marshmallows and making s'mores. In case you are not familiar with s'mores, let me help you. S'mores are a kind of cookie sandwich made up of marshmallows, plain (semi-sweet) chocolate and graham crackers. The name comes from a contraction of 'some more'. Need I say more? Pictured page 48.

MAKES 15

1 x quantity Graham Cracker Slice-and-bake Cookies (see page 46)

15 pieces of plain (semi-sweet) chocolate

15 large marshmallows, toasted

1. Take a cookie and place a piece of chocolate on top followed by a hot, toasted marshmallow, which will begin to melt the chocolate.
2. Add a second cookie on top, if desired, and enjoy immediately!

Tahini-filled variation Graham cracker cookies are also delicious filled with Tahini Frosting (see page 207) or Chocolate Frosting (see page 207). Use a butter knife or a piping (pastry) bag to spread some filling onto a graham cracker cookie and top with a second one to make a delicious sandwich! If you're feeling particularly decadent, drizzle some Miso Caramel with Sea Salt (see page 203) on top of the filling before adding the second cookie. Good Lord!

OAT SHORTBREAD

I visited a friend while writing this book and took some shortbread with me. My friend said he loved it. I, however, felt it was missing a little something. He described the time he'd eaten shortbread with a whisky tasting – a savoury shortbread with fennel. Bingo!

MAKES 20

200g (scant 1½ cups) plain (all-purpose) flour

100g (½ cup) oat flour (you can make oat flour by grinding oats in a food processor until very fine)

¼ tsp vanilla salt (see page 202) or salt

200g (1¾ sticks) butter, softened

50g (⅓ cup) light muscovado sugar

50g (scant ½ cup) icing (confectioners') sugar

For topping

½ tsp fennel seeds, finely ground

¼ tsp vanilla salt (see page 202) or salt

1 tbsp caster (superfine) sugar

1. In a large bowl, combine the flours with the vanilla salt or salt. Set aside.
2. Using a stand mixer or hand-held electric whisk, cream together the butter and sugars for several minutes until light and fluffy. Add the flours and salt, and mix to combine. Gently knead the dough together by hand. Do not overmix.
3. Shape the dough into a 4cm (1½in) diameter round log or into a rectangle about 2cm (¾in) thick and 6cm (2¼in) deep. At this stage, you can wrap the dough in parchment and refrigerate for up to 1 week.
4. When ready to bake, preheat the oven to 160°C fan (325°F/Gas 3) and line a baking sheet with parchment. Combine the ingredients for topping.
5. Cut 1cm (½in) thick slices from the rectangle or log and place on the lined baking sheet. Use a fork or cocktail stick (toothpick) to prick the dough to form a pattern and sprinkle with the fennel/salt/sugar mixture before baking.
6. Bake in the preheated oven for 17–18 minutes until just golden. Let cool completely on the baking sheet (while warm, the shortbreads are very delicate).

Petticoat Tails Roll one-quarter of the dough into a 12cm (5in) diameter disc, 1cm (½in) thick, directly onto the baking sheet. Prick with a fork and score into eight wedges. Once cooked, cool on the baking sheet for 5 minutes, then cut into triangles.

Chill
The dough can be kept in the fridge, wrapped airtight, for 1 week.

Freeze
The dough can either be frozen as a log or as sliced cookies for up to 6 months. Simply wrap airtight and freeze.

Bake from frozen
Preheat the oven as above. Bake cookie slices on a lined baking sheet for 17–18 minutes. Let a frozen log of dough thaw enough to slice, then bake as above.

COOKIES

NUTTY CITRUS SHORTBREAD

Cashews, almonds and pistachios all combine well with citrus zest. If you can't decide which to use, use a mixture! And remember, rice flour is the key to delicate shortbread.

MAKES 20

200g (scant 1½ cups) plain (all-purpose) flour

100g (generous ¾ cup) rice flour

100g (¾ cup) roasted and lightly salted nuts, such as cashews, skinned almonds or pistachios, finely chopped

¼ tsp vanilla salt (see page 202) or salt

finely grated zest of 1 lemon and ½ orange or lime

100g (½ cup) caster (granulated) sugar

200g (1¾ sticks) butter, softened

For topping

1 tbsp caster (superfine) sugar

¼ tsp vanilla salt (see page 202) or salt

1. In a large bowl, combine the flours, chopped nuts, vanilla salt or salt and zests. Set aside.
2. Using a stand mixer or hand-held electric whisk, cream together the sugar and butter for several minutes until light and fluffy. Beat in the flour mixture just to combine, then knead the dough together by hand. It can be a bit dry, but this is correct!
3. Shape the dough into a 4cm (1½in) diameter round log or into a rectangle about 2cm (¾in) thick and 6cm (2¼in) deep. Wrap the dough in parchment and refrigerate for at least 1 hour.
4. When ready to bake, preheat the oven to 160°C fan (325°F/Gas 3) and line a baking sheet with parchment. Combine the sugar with the vanilla salt or salt.
5. With a very sharp knife, cut 1cm (½in) thick slices from the rectangle or log and place on the lined baking sheet. Use a fork or cocktail stick (toothpick) to prick the dough to form a pattern, and sprinkle with the sugar and salt mixture.
6. Bake in the preheated oven for 17–18 minutes, or until just golden. Let cool completely on the baking sheet before removing. While warm, the shortbreads are still very delicate.

Petticoat Tails See page 51.

Chill
The dough can be kept in the fridge, wrapped airtight, for 1 week.

Freeze
The dough can either be frozen as a log, rectangle or as sliced rounds for up to 6 months. Simply wrap airtight and freeze.

Bake from frozen
Preheat the oven as above. Bake cookie slices on a lined baking sheet for 17–18 minutes. Let a frozen log of dough thaw enough to slice, then bake as above.

COOKIES

CAKE

IES

CAKE-IES are very special to me. Whenever I begin working on a new idea, I dream about it. I work through the 'kinks' in my sleep. My vision was a hybrid bake with the texture of cake but the shape and size of a cookie. No baking pan, no cupcake liner, you need just some heat and a baking sheet.

A HYBRID BAKE WITH THE TEXTURE OF CAKE BUT THE SHAPE AND SIZE OF A COOKIE

THE ULTIMATE IN CAKE-EASE

Cake-ies are at the heart of batch baking: their batters are easy to make, versatile, and forgiving. Whip up some cake-ie batter in minutes and keep it in the fridge for *days*. Simply bake the amount you want to eat, right when you want it. You can even use the batter to bake one large snacking cake. Or freeze the batter in portions and bake them… **in 6 months!**

They can be savoury, sweet, vegan or gluten- free. Dress a cake-ie up with a dusting of icing (confectioners') sugar or leave it plain. The savoury ones are delicious with butter, as a side with some soup or salad. You can even double up and make cake-ie sandwiches with a tasty frosting filling. Save time by making a batter that patiently waits for you in the fridge. Need a last-minute party dessert? A pick-me-up after a rough day? A breakfast on the run? No need to start from scratch every time you want to bake.

Here's what you need for cake-ies
- airtight container for the batter
- baking sheet
- some parchment
- ice cream scoop – I have two sizes: 4cm (1½in) diameter and 5cm (2in) diameter
- 23cm (9in) square baking pan in case you feel like baking a snacking cake
- 15cm (6in) or 23cm (9in) round baking pan if you fancy baking a tiered cake

If I were a cake-ie, what would I say?
'I forgive you. You forgot about me in the freezer 5 months ago. Just preheat the oven and pop me in.'

What else?
'I noticed you were ravenous when you got home from work. I am waiting for you in the fridge. Just scoop me out, throw me in the oven and before you know it, I'm at the table with you and the world is a peaceful place again.'

A final word…
'It's Sunday. Junior needs a birthday cake next Saturday and this is the busiest week of your life. I'm a large cake, bake *me*! You can freeze me, then thaw me and spruce me up so I'm ready to go.'

SPICED SWEET POTATO CAKE-IES

I love savoury baking, especially with these cake-ies. A perfect, quick afternoon snack when you don't want a sugar rush. With soup or salad, these cake-ies complete a tasty meal.

MAKES 20

300g (10½oz) sweet potatoes

2 tbsp olive oil

½ tsp sea salt

½ tsp ground cumin

280g (2 cups) plain (all-purpose) flour

2 tsp baking powder

1 tsp bicarbonate of soda (baking soda)

1 tsp caster (granulated) sugar

¼ tsp salt

50ml (3½ tbsp) olive oil

250g (generous 1 cup) Greek yogurt or sour cream

150ml (scant ⅔ cup) whole milk

1 egg

75g (1 cup) coarsely grated Manchego cheese

100g (¾ cup) soft goat's cheese or feta, crumbled

30g (3 tbsp) pepitas (pumpkin seeds), toasted, cooled and coarsely chopped

50g (⅓ cup) dried cranberries

4 tbsp finely chopped fresh herbs, such as parsley, lemon thyme or tarragon

1 chilli, finely chopped

grated zest of 1 lemon

coarsely ground black pepper

1. Preheat the oven to 225°C fan (430°F/Gas 7) and line a baking sheet with parchment. Cut the sweet potatoes into 1.5cm (⅝in) cubes. Place in a bowl and coat with the olive oil, sea salt and cumin, then arrange on the baking sheet.

2. Roast in the preheated oven for 15–18 minutes until beginning to caramelize. Let cool on the baking sheet, then transfer to a bowl.

3. Combine the flour, baking powder, bicarbonate of soda (baking soda), sugar and salt in a bowl. Set aside. Beat together the oil, yogurt, milk and egg. Set aside.

4. Combine the cheeses, pepitas, dried cranberries, herbs, chilli, lemon zest and some coarsely ground pepper with the roasted vegetables.

5. Gently but thoroughly stir the oil, yogurt, milk and egg into the flour. Add the roasted vegetable mixture and stir to combine. Do not overmix.

6. Transfer the batter to an airtight container and let it rest in the fridge for 2 hours.

7. When ready to bake, preheat the oven to 195°C fan (380°F/Gas 5) and line a baking sheet with parchment.

8. Using an ice cream scoop or a tablespoon, place mounds of batter 5cm (2in) apart on the lined baking sheet. Bake in the preheated oven for 14 minutes until golden and the cake-ies spring back when lightly touched.

Chill
The batter can be kept in the fridge in an airtight container for up to 3 days.

Freeze
Simply freeze mounds of batter on a plate. Once frozen, wrap airtight and freeze for up to 6 months.

Bake from frozen
Preheat the oven as above and bake the cake-ies on a lined baking sheet for 15–17 minutes until golden.

FLORENTINE CAKE-IES

These herby, cheesy, savoury spinach cake-ies are lovely topped with savoury streusel. If you are going to freeze them, make sure you top them with the streusel before freezing, otherwise the streusel won't adhere to the frozen batter.

MAKES 20

100g (½ cup) cooked spinach (400g/14oz fresh weight), drained and finely chopped or 150g/5oz frozen, chopped spinach, thawed and well drained

200g (scant 1½ cups) plain (all-purpose) flour

75g (scant ½ cup) coarse polenta (cornmeal) (do not use instant polenta)

3 tsp baking powder

1 tsp caster (granulated) sugar

½ tsp salt

50ml (3½ tbsp) olive oil

175ml (¾ cup) whole milk

1 egg

250g (9oz/generous 1 cup) ricotta cheese

50g (⅔ cup) grated Parmesan cheese

3 tbsp pine nuts or mixed nuts

handful of fresh herbs (such as basil, parsley and thyme), finely chopped (about 4 tbsp chopped)

1 chilli, finely chopped, or some coarsely ground black pepper

grated zest of 1 lemon

1 x quantity Savoury Streusel (optional, see page 211)

1. Squeeze all the excess liquid from the cooked spinach. Set aside.
2. In a large bowl, combine the flour, polenta (cornmeal), baking powder, sugar and salt. Set aside. Using a whisk, beat together the oil, milk and egg. Set aside.
3. Combine the ricotta, Parmesan, nuts, herbs, chilli and lemon zest with the prepared spinach. Gently but thoroughly stir in the oil, milk and egg mixture.
4. Add the flour mixture to the spinach mixture and stir to combine. Do not overmix.
5. Transfer the batter to an airtight container and let it rest in the fridge for 2 hours.
6. When ready to bake, preheat the oven to 195°C fan (380°F/Gas 5) and line a baking sheet with parchment.
7. Using an ice cream scoop or a tablespoon, place mounds of batter 5cm (2in) apart on the lined baking sheet. Top with savoury breadcrumb-cheese streusel, if using.
8. Bake in the preheated oven for 14–16 minutes, or until golden and the cake-ies spring back when lightly touched.

Chill

The batter can be kept in the fridge in an airtight container for up to 3 days.

Freeze

Simply freeze mounds of streusel-topped batter on a plate. Once frozen, wrap airtight and freeze for up to 6 months.

Bake from frozen

Preheat the oven as above and bake on a lined baking sheet for about 16–17 minutes, or until golden.

CAKE-IES

CORN CAKE-IES WITH CHEESE AND CHILLIES

I was born on the West Coast of America, but went to boarding school on the East Coast. For some reason, perhaps because my mother was Canadian, I wasn't introduced to cornbread until one day a student surprised me with an entire pan of her Mom's. A sense memory like no other, this is my ode to Kirsten and her mother. Enjoy!

MAKES 20

140g (1 cup) plain (all-purpose) flour

140g (generous ¾ cup) coarse polenta (cornmeal) (do not use instant polenta)

1 tbsp caster (granulated) sugar

2 tsp baking powder

½ tsp bicarbonate of soda (baking soda)

1¼ tsp salt

150g (generous 1 cup) sweetcorn (corn kernals), fresh, frozen and thawed, or canned and well drained

130g (1½ cups) coarsely grated Cheddar cheese

1 chilli, chopped

1–2 tbsp finely chopped mixed fresh herbs, such as parsley, basil, thyme or sage

250ml (1 cup) buttermilk

1 egg

60g (½ stick) butter, melted and cooled

2 tbsp olive oil

1. In a large bowl, combine the flour, polenta (cornmeal), sugar, baking powder, bicarbonate of soda (baking soda) and salt. Set aside.
2. In a separate bowl, combine the corn, cheese, chilli and herbs. Set aside.
3. Using a whisk, beat together the buttermilk, egg, melted butter and olive oil. Add this liquid mixture to the flour mixture and stir to barely combine.
4. Gently mix in the cheese, corn, chilli and fresh herbs. Do not overmix.
5. Transfer the batter to an airtight container and let rest in the fridge for 30 minutes.
6. When ready to bake, preheat the oven to 200°C fan (400°F/Gas 6) and line a baking sheet with parchment. Using an ice cream scoop or a tablespoon, place mounds of batter 5cm (2in) apart onto the baking sheet.
7. Bake in the preheated oven for 18 minutes, or until golden and the cake-ies spring back when lightly touched. Let cool on the baking sheet for 10 minutes before transferring to a wire rack to cool completely.

Chill
The batter can be kept in the fridge in an airtight container for up to 3 days.

Freeze
Simply freeze mounds of batter on a plate. Once frozen, wrap airtight and freeze for up to 6 months.

Bake from frozen
Preheat the oven as above and bake on a lined baking sheet for about 19–20 minutes, or until golden.

BROWNIE CAKE-IES

In a baking-world according to me, brownies must be soft in the middle, very chocolate-y, and have a very thin crust on the surface. Voilà!

MAKES 20-25

45g (3 tbsp) butter

200g (7oz) plain (semi-sweet) chocolate, chopped

4 tbsp olive or vegetable oil

50g (½ cup) unsweetened cocoa powder

90g (⅔ cup) plain (all-purpose) flour

½ tsp baking powder

¾ tsp vanilla salt (see page 202) or salt

75g (6 tbsp) caster (granulated) sugar

100g (⅔ cup) dark brown muscovado sugar

2 eggs, room temperature

1 tbsp vanilla extract (see page 202)

3 tbsp whole milk

100g (3½oz) white or plain (semi-sweet) chocolate, coarsely chopped (optional)

1. In a small pan, melt the butter. Remove from the heat, add the chopped chocolate and stir to melt. Whisk in the oil and cocoa powder, and set aside.
2. In a small bowl combine the flour, baking powder and vanilla salt or salt.
3. In a stand mixer or a large bowl, whisk together the sugars, eggs and vanilla extract. Beat vigorously for 4–5 minutes until light and airy. Add the butter and chocolate mixture and the milk. Whisk to combine well.
4. With a rubber spatula, stir in the flour mixture followed by the chopped chocolate.
5. Transfer the batter to an airtight container and refrigerate for at least 2 hours.
6. When ready to bake, preheat the oven to 175°C fan (350°F/Gas 4) and line a baking sheet with parchment.
7. Using an ice cream scoop or a tablespoon, place mounds of batter onto the lined baking sheet about 5cm (2in) apart. Slightly flatten with the palm of your hand before baking.
8. Bake in the preheated oven for about 10 minutes, or until the cake-ies spring back when lightly touched. Do not overbake. Let cool on the baking sheet for 10 minutes, then transfer to a wire rack to cool completely.

Chill
The batter can be kept in the fridge in an airtight container for up to 7 days.

Freeze
Simply freeze mounds of batter on a plate. Once frozen, wrap airtight and freeze for up to 6 months.

Bake from frozen
Preheat the oven as above and bake on a lined baking sheet for 12–14 minutes, or until the cake-ies spring back when lightly touched.

BANANA CAKE-IES

I grew up baking banana bread. It was a Friday night staple in my 9-year-old baking repertoire. So it just made sense to develop a vegan version. Thankfully I've been able to expand my schedule and this recipe is no longer limited to Friday nights.

MAKES 20

VEGAN

1 tbsp ground linseeds (flaxseeds)

3 tbsp hot water

200g (7oz) bananas (2–3 ripe bananas)

1 tbsp freshly squeezed lemon juice

250g (1¾ cups) plain (all-purpose) flour

1 tsp bicarbonate of soda (baking soda)

1 tsp baking powder

½ tsp ground cinnamon

¼ tsp ground nutmeg

½ tsp vanilla salt (see page 202) or salt

75g (⅓ cup) Demerara (raw) sugar or 75g (½ cup) light soft brown sugar

100ml (scant ½ cup) vegetable oil

2 tsp vanilla extract (see page 202)

Plus 150–175g (5½–6oz) extra ingredients, chosen from:

50g (scant ½ cup) walnut halves or macadamia nuts, coarsely chopped

50g (generous ⅓ cup) dried cranberries or dried cherries, or chopped dates

50g (scant ⅓ cup) raisins

75g (½ cup) finely chopped vegan chocolate of your choice

1. Begin by mixing the ground linseeds (flaxseeds) with the hot water. Let sit for about 10 minutes in the fridge until it becomes gelatinous.
2. Mash the bananas to a fine purée and stir in the lemon juice. Set aside.
3. In a large bowl, combine the flour, bicarbonate of soda (baking soda), baking powder, spices and vanilla salt or salt. In a separate bowl, combine the desired extra ingredients.
4. In another large bowl, whisk together the sugar and oil. Add the vanilla, linseed (flaxseed) mixture and banana purée. Using a spatula or wooden spoon, stir in the flour mixture and the desired extra ingredients. Mix to combine. Do not overmix.
5. Transfer the batter to an airtight container and refrigerate for at least 2 hours.
6. When ready to bake, preheat the oven to 185°C fan (365°F/Gas 4) and line a baking sheet with parchment. Using an ice cream scoop or a tablespoon, spoon mounds of batter onto the lined baking sheet, about 5cm (2in) apart.
7. Bake in the preheated oven for about 12 minutes, or until golden and the cake-ies spring back when lightly touched. Transfer to a wire rack to cool.

Chill

The batter can be kept in the fridge in an airtight container for up to 4 days.

Freeze

Simply freeze mounds of batter on a plate. Once frozen, wrap airtight and freeze for up to 6 months.

Bake from frozen

Preheat the oven as above and bake on a lined baking sheet for about 14–16 minutes, or until golden.

CHOCOLATE HAZELNUT CAKE-IES

These gluten-free cake-ies are a cross between a molten-lava cake and homemade hazelnut spread. Make sure to bake them only until they are set. The longer you bake them, the more cake-like the consistency will become. I like them a bit gooey on the inside.

MAKES 16–20

GLUTEN-FREE

125g (1 stick) butter

200g (7oz) plain (semi-sweet) chocolate, coarsely chopped

100g (¾ cup) hazelnuts, skinned, finely ground and lightly toasted (see note)

35g (⅓ cup) unsweetened cocoa powder, sifted

¼ tsp vanilla salt (see page 202) or salt

¼ tsp baking powder

3 eggs, room temperature (very important)

135g (scant 1 cup) dark brown muscovado sugar

1 tsp vanilla extract (see page 202)

To serve (optional)

3 tbsp icing (confectioners') sugar, sifted

200ml (¾ cup plus 1½ tbsp) double (heavy) cream, cold

½ tsp ground cinnamon

1. Melt the butter in a small pan. Remove from the heat, add the chocolate and stir to melt. Set aside. In a medium bowl, combine the finely ground hazelnuts with the cocoa, vanilla salt or salt and baking powder. Set aside.

2. Using a stand mixer or hand-held electric whisk, beat the eggs and sugar on high speed for 8 minutes until the mixture forms ribbons. Whisk in the vanilla extract and melted butter and chocolate mixture and combine well. Fold in the nut mixture.

3. Transfer the batter to an airtight container and refrigerate for at least 1 hour.

4. When ready to bake, preheat the oven to 180°C fan (350°F/Gas 4) and line a baking sheet with parchment.

5. Using an ice cream scoop or a tablespoon, scoop out mounds of batter onto the lined baking sheet about 5cm (2in) apart.

6. Bake in the preheated oven for about 8 minutes. Do not overbake.

7. Let cool on the baking sheet; they will be too delicate to move when hot, but will set when cooled.

8. Serve plain, dusted with icing (confectioners') sugar, or whip the cream with the cinnamon and serve with a dollop of cinnamon whipped cream.

Note This gluten-free batter also works well with chestnut flour. There is no need to toast the chestnut flour.

Chill
The batter can be kept in the fridge in an airtight container for up to 7 days.

Freeze
Simply freeze mounds of batter on a plate. Once frozen, wrap airtight and freeze for up to 6 months.

Bake from frozen
Preheat the oven as above and bake on a lined baking sheet for 8–9 minutes until set.

VEGAN CHOCOLATE CAKE-IES

These cake-ies are the perfect canvas for all your ideas. Try a speedy version with a simple dusting of cocoa or icing (confectioners') sugar. Or… you can up your game and top with Vegan Ermine Frosting (see page 205) and top the cake-ie with a berry or some grated vegan chocolate.

MAKES 16

VEGAN

125ml (½ cup) plant-based milk, such as pea protein, cashew or oat milk etc.

1 tsp any vinegar

150g (scant ⅔ cup) apple sauce

100ml (scant ½ cup) vegetable oil

1 tbsp vanilla extract (see page 202)

125g (¾ cup) light muscovado sugar or 125g (scant ⅔ cup) Demerara (raw) sugar

175g (1¼ cups) plain (all-purpose) flour

60g (⅔ cup) unsweetened cocoa powder, sifted

1 tsp bicarbonate of soda (baking soda)

1 tsp baking powder

½ tsp salt

1 tsp instant espresso powder (optional)

1. Beat together the plant-based milk, vinegar, apple sauce, vegetable oil and vanilla extract in a bowl. Set aside.
2. In a large bowl, combine the sugar, flour, cocoa, bicarbonate of soda (baking soda), baking powder and salt. Add the instant espresso powder, if using. Add the wet ingredients to the flour mixture and combine well. Do not overmix.
3. Transfer the batter to an airtight container and refrigerate for at least 2 hours.
4. When ready to bake, preheat the oven to 180°C fan (350°F/Gas 4) and line a baking sheet with parchment.
5. Using an ice cream scoop or a tablespoon, place mounds of batter 5cm (2in) apart on the lined baking sheet.
6. Bake in the preheated oven for 11 minutes, or until the cake-ies have puffed up and spring back when lightly touched.
7. Let cool on the baking sheet for 10 minutes before transferring to a wire rack to cool completely.

Tip Top with Vegan Ermine Frosting (see page 205).

Chill
The batter can be kept in the fridge in an airtight container for up to 5 days.

Freeze
Simply freeze mounds of batter on a plate. Once frozen, wrap airtight and freeze for up to 6 months.

Bake from frozen
Preheat the oven as above and bake on a lined baking sheet for 12–13 minutes, or until the cake-ies spring back when lightly touched.

LEMON CAKE-IES WITH QUARK AND ALMONDS

I have been living for most of my adult life in Germany. Although I have written eight cookbooks, this is my first recipe with quark, a fresh curd cheese common in German cuisine. As we all know, home is where the heart is, and my heart is in Berlin. *Jawohl*!

MAKES 24

180g (1⅓ cups) plain (all-purpose) flour

100g (1 cup) finely ground almonds

2 tsp baking powder

½ tsp bicarbonate of soda (baking soda)

¾ tsp vanilla salt (see page 202) or salt

½ tsp ground star anise (optional, but delicious!)

2 eggs, room temperature

110g (generous ½ cup) caster (granulated) sugar

250g (generous 1 cup) quark (40%) or ricotta cheese, well drained

grated zest of 1 lemon

50ml (3½ tbsp) freshly squeezed lemon juice

100g (1 cup) flaked (sliced) almonds (optional)

1. Whisk together the flour, ground almonds, baking powder, bicarbonate of soda (baking soda), vanilla salt or salt and star anise, if using. Set aside.
2. In a large bowl, beat the eggs with the sugar for 5–7 minutes until thick, pale and creamy. Beat in the quark or ricotta, followed by the lemon zest and lemon juice. Fold in the flour/almond mixture and stir until just combined.
3. Transfer the batter to an airtight container and refrigerate for at least 2 hours.
4. When ready to bake, preheat the oven to 180°C fan (350°F/Gas 4) and line a baking sheet with parchment.
5. Using an ice cream scoop or a tablespoon, place mounds of batter 5cm (2in) apart on the lined baking sheet. Gently press some flaked (sliced) almonds onto the cake-ies, if desired.
6. Bake in the preheated oven for 10 minutes, or until lightly golden. Do not overbake.
7. Let cool on the baking sheet for 10 minutes before transferring to a wire rack to cool completely.

Chill
The batter can be kept in the fridge in an airtight container for up to 3 days.

Freeze
Simply freeze mounds of batter on a plate, with or without flaked (sliced) almonds. Once frozen, wrap airtight and freeze for up to 6 months.

Bake from frozen
Preheat the oven as above and bake on a lined baking sheet for 10–11 minutes, or until the cake-ies are golden.

VEGAN LEMON CAKE-IES

These cake-ies are simply delightful! The citrus zests bring out the flavour of the almonds and the flax-eggs complement the nuttiness of the marzipan and ensure a light texture.

MAKES 20

VEGAN

1 tbsp ground linseeds (flaxseeds)

3 tbsp hot water

grated zest of 1 lemon

grated zest of 1 orange

100ml (scant ½ cup) plant-based milk, such as pea protein or cashew

2 tsp freshly squeezed lemon juice

1 tbsp vanilla extract (see page 202)

250g (1¾ cups) plain (all-purpose) flour

100g (1 cup) finely ground almonds

2 tsp baking powder

1 tsp bicarbonate of soda (baking soda)

¾ tsp vanilla salt (see page 202) or salt

1 tsp ground cardamom

200g (7oz) marzipan, broken up

150g (scant ⅔ cup) apple sauce

100ml (scant ½ cup) vegetable oil

75g (6 tbsp) caster (granulated) sugar

For topping

2 tbsp Demerara (raw) sugar

4 tbsp flaked (sliced) almonds

1. Begin by mixing the ground linseeds (flaxseeds) with the hot water. Let sit for about 10 minutes in the fridge until it becomes gelatinous.
2. Combine the lemon and orange zest, plant-based milk, lemon juice and vanilla extract. Set aside. In a large bowl, combine the flour, ground almonds, baking powder, bicarbonate of soda (baking soda), vanilla salt or salt and cardamom.
3. Using a stand mixer or hand-held electric whisk, beat the marzipan with the apple sauce. Beat in the vegetable oil and sugar. Continue to beat until smooth. Stir in the milk mixture, followed by the flour mixture. Do not overmix.
4. Transfer the batter to an airtight container and refrigerate for at least 2 hours.
5. When ready to bake, preheat the oven to 180°C fan (350°F/Gas 4) and line a baking sheet with parchment.
6. Using an ice cream scoop or a tablespoon, place mounds of the batter 5cm (2in) apart on the baking sheet. Sprinkle over the sugar and almonds for topping.
7. Bake in the preheated oven for 11 minutes, or until golden, puffed up and the cake-ies spring back when lightly touched. Let cool on the baking sheet for 10 minutes before transferring to a wire rack to cool completely.

Chill

The batter can be stored in an airtight container in the fridge for up to 5 days.

Freeze

Simply freeze mounds of sugar and almond-topped batter on a plate. Once frozen, wrap airtight and freeze for up to 6 months.

Bake from frozen

Preheat the oven as above and bake on a lined baking sheet for about 14–16 minutes, or until golden.

VANILLA CAKE-IES WITH CURRANTS

These little cake-ies are a twist on a cupcake that my grandmother used to make when I was growing up. Beautiful in its simplicity – no frosting, no buttercream – I even took it a step further and stripped the cake-ie of its cupcake liner. I love minimalism.

MAKES 25

200g (scant 1½ cups) plain (all-purpose) flour

50g (scant ½ cup) cornflour (cornstarch)

2½ tsp baking powder

½ tsp bicarbonate of soda (baking soda)

¾ tsp vanilla salt (see page 202) or salt

100g (¾ cup) currants

150g (¾ cup) caster (granulated) sugar

125g (1 stick) butter, softened

2 eggs, room temperature

1 tsp vanilla extract (see page 202)

100ml (scant ½ cup) buttermilk (or 100ml/scant ½ cup whole milk plus ½ tsp vinegar)

1. Whisk together the flour, cornflour (cornstarch), baking powder, bicarbonate of soda (baking soda) and vanilla salt or salt. Add the currants. Set aside.
2. In a large bowl, beat the sugar with the butter and eggs for 6–8 minutes until thick and creamy.
3. Beat in the vanilla extract and buttermilk.
4. Fold in the flour mixture and stir until just combined.
5. Transfer the batter to an airtight container and refrigerate for at least 2 hours.
6. When ready to bake, preheat the oven to 180°C fan (350°F/Gas 4) and line a baking sheet with parchment.
7. Using an ice cream scoop or a tablespoon, place mounds of batter 5cm (2in) apart on the lined baking sheet.
8. Bake in the preheated oven for 12 minutes, or until lightly golden. Do not overbake.
9. Let cool on the baking sheet for 10 minutes before transferring to a wire rack to cool completely.

Chill

The batter can be kept in the fridge in an airtight container for up to 4 days.

Freeze

Simply freeze mounds of batter on a plate. Once frozen, wrap airtight and freeze for up to 6 months.

Bake from frozen

Preheat the oven as above and bake on a lined baking sheet for 13–14 minutes, or until the cake-ies are golden.

CARROT CAKE-IES

I first had carrot cake in Greenwich Village when I was a teenager and on 'leave' from boarding school with my best friend. This was the 80s and our decadence knew no bounds. Foot-loose and fancy-free, we rode horses in Central Park, drank Kahlua and milk, partied at Max's Kansas City, and ate carrot cake for breakfast. Max's is closed now, no more horseback riding in the Park, and I can't imagine enjoying a milk-based cocktail, but a vegan carrot cake is nothing short of inspired!

MAKES 24

VEGAN

275g (2 cups) plain (all-purpose) flour

200g (1 cup) caster (granulated) sugar

1 tsp bicarbonate of soda (baking soda)

1 tsp baking powder

1 tsp ground cinnamon

½ tsp salt

100g (¾ cup) walnut halves, coarsely chopped

75g (¾ cup) desiccated (dried unsweetened shredded) coconut

75g (½ cup) raisins

200g (1⅓ cups) coarsely grated carrots

175g (¾ cup) apple sauce

175ml (¾ cup) vegetable oil

125ml (½ cup) pineapple juice

For topping

grated zest of 1 lemon

1 x quantity Vegan Ermine Frosting (see page 205)

1. Whisk together the flour, sugar, bicarbonate of soda (baking soda), baking powder, cinnamon and salt. Set aside.
2. In another bowl, combine the walnuts with the coconut, raisins and grated carrots.
3. In another bowl or jug (cup), whisk together the apple sauce and vegetable oil. Beat in the pineapple juice.
4. Using a rubber spatula, add the wet ingredients to the flour mixture and stir to barely combine. Fold in the carrot mixture.
5. Transfer the batter to an airtight container and refrigerate for at least 1 hour.
6. When ready to bake, preheat the oven to 175°C fan (350°F/Gas 4) and line a baking sheet with parchment. Using an ice cream scoop or a tablespoon, place mounds of the batter 5cm (2in) apart on the lined baking sheet.
7. Bake in the preheated oven for 17–19 minutes, or until golden. Do not overbake. Transfer to a wire rack to cool.
8. Beat the lemon zest into the ermine frosting and use to decorate the cake-ies.

Chill

The batter can be kept in the fridge in an airtight container for up to 5 days.

Freeze

Simply freeze mounds of batter on a plate. Once frozen, wrap airtight and freeze for up to 6 months.

Bake from frozen

Preheat the oven as above and bake on a lined baking sheet for about 18–20 minutes, or until golden.

CHOCOLATE SNACKING CAKE

I get it. Been there, done that – the last-minute birthday cake… or the cake planned 5 days in advance because of a busy week. Here it is. Make it plant-based, make it classic, make it in advance to freeze and thaw. It is delicious with Swiss Meringue Buttercream (see page 210), Chocolate Frosting or Tahini Frosting (see page 207).

MAKES 1 CAKE

VEGAN OPTION

100g (⅔ cup) plain (semi-sweet) chocolate, broken up

200ml (¾ cup plus 1½ tbsp) boiling water

60g (⅔ cup) unsweetened cocoa powder

150g (1 cup plus 2 tbsp) plain (all-purpose) flour

50g (⅓ cup plus 2 tbsp) cornflour (cornstarch)

1 tsp bicarbonate of soda (baking soda)

½ tsp baking powder

¾ tsp vanilla salt (see page 202) or salt

150g (¾ cup) caster (granulated) sugar or brown sugar

100ml (scant ½ cup) vegetable oil

2 eggs (or use 100g/ generous ⅓ cup apple sauce for plant-based)

150ml (⅔ cup) buttermilk (or use 150ml/⅔ cup plant-based milk plus 1 tsp vinegar for plant-based)

1½ tsp vanilla extract (see page 202)

1. Preheat the oven to 180°C fan (350°F/Gas 4) and grease a 23cm (9in) square or 25cm (10in) round baking pan.
2. In a measuring jug (cup), combine the chocolate with the hot water. Stir until the chocolate is melted and the mixture is smooth. Whisk in the cocoa until all lumps are dissolved. Let cool. Sift the flour, cornflour (cornstarch), bicarbonate of soda (baking soda), baking powder and vanilla salt or salt into a bowl. Set aside.
3. In large bowl, whisk together the sugar and oil. Add the eggs one at a time (or the apple sauce for a plant-based cake) and continue to beat until well mixed. Add the buttermilk (or plant-based milk and vinegar), vanilla extract and cooled melted chocolate mixture, beating until well combined.
4. Stir in the dry ingredients and mix well to combine. This is a rather wet batter.
5. Pour the batter into the prepared baking pan and bake in the preheated oven for 25–30 minutes, or until a cocktail stick (toothpick) comes out clean. Allow to cool in the pan for 10 minutes before turning out onto a wire rack to cool completely before frosting or freezing.

Tip You can double the recipe to bake a layer cake.

Chill
The cake will keep in the fridge, wrapped airtight, for up to 5 days.

Freeze
Once completely cooled, wrap airtight (unfrosted) and freeze for 6 months.

Defrost
Let thaw overnight in the fridge or on the kitchen counter for a few hours.

CAKE-IES

SEMI-NAKED VANILLA CAKE

This plant-based cake recipe looks lovely covered thinly with vegan frosting.
Here, I have used half of the batter to make a four-tiered 15cm (6in) cake, but
you can use the whole thing to make a two-tiered 23cm (9in) round cake or a
24 x 32cm (9½ x 12½in) snacking cake.

MAKES 1 CAKE

VEGAN

500g (generous 3½ cups) plain (all-purpose) flour

100g (¾ cup) cornflour (cornstarch) or finely ground almonds

2 tsp baking powder

2 tsp bicarbonate of soda (baking soda)

1 tsp vanilla salt (see page 202) or salt

350g (1¾ cups) caster (granulated) sugar

450ml (1¾ cups plus 2 tbsp) oat milk or other unsweetened plant-based milk

2 tsp light, colourless vinegar

grated zest of 1 orange or lemon

100g (generous ⅓ cup) apple sauce

1 tbsp vanilla extract (see page 202)

vegan margarine, for greasing

For filling and topping

1 x quantity Vegan Ermine Frosting (see page 205)

fresh, edible flowers or berries, depending on the season, to decorate

1. Preheat the oven to 170°C fan (325°F/Gas 3) and lightly grease two 15cm (6in) round cake pans with margarine.
2. In a large bowl, combine the flour, cornflour (cornstarch), baking powder, bicarbonate of soda (baking soda), vanilla salt or salt and sugar. Set aside.
3. Whisk together the oat milk, vinegar, citrus zest, apple sauce and vanilla extract.
4. Stir the oat milk mixture into the flour mixture. Do not overmix.
5. Distribute half the batter evenly between the baking pans. Bake in the preheated oven for 26–29 minutes until a cocktail stick (toothpick) inserted into the cake comes out clean. Let cool in the pans for 10 minutes, then turn out onto a wire rack to cool completely.
6. Slice off the tops off the cakes to create a flat surface, then use a serrated knife to slice each cake into two layers. Place the first cake on a plate. Spread with a little ermine frosting and, if desired, sprinkle with berries. Place the second cake, cut-side down, on top. Press down lightly. Repeat with the third and fourth layers.
7. Cover the sides of the cake with a thin coating of the ermine frosting. Spread or pipe a thicker layer of frosting on top. Decorate with edible flowers or berries.

Chill
The bases will keep in the fridge, wrapped airtight, for up to 5 days.

Freeze
Once completely cooled, wrap airtight (unfrosted) and freeze for 6 months.

Defrost
Let thaw overnight in the fridge or on the kitchen counter for a few hours.

CHOCOLATE SAUERKRAUT CAKE

This uber-global recipe unites sauerkraut, a national German dish, with the ideal American chocolate cake. The acidity of the sauerkraut highlights the intense chocolate flavour and gives it a fluffy texture. The cake batter is also perfect for making cake-ies.

MAKES 1 CAKE

210g (1½ cups) plain (all-purpose) flour

65g (⅔ cup) unsweetened cocoa powder, sifted

½ tsp baking powder

½ tsp bicarbonate of soda (baking soda)

¼ tsp vanilla salt (see page 202) or salt

100g (6½ tbsp) butter, softened

175g (1 cup minus 2 tbsp) caster (granulated) sugar

2 eggs, room temperature

½ tsp vanilla extract (see page 202)

125ml (½ cup) water

75g (2½oz) sauerkraut, rinsed and finely chopped

1⅓ x quantity Chocolate Frosting (page 207)

1. Preheat the oven to 175°C fan (350°F/Gas 4) and lightly butter two 15cm (6in) baking pans.
2. In a large bowl, combine the flour, cocoa, baking powder, bicarbonate of soda (baking soda) and vanilla salt or salt.
3. Using a stand mixer or hand-held electric whisk, whip the butter and sugar until creamy. Add the eggs and vanilla extract. Continue to beat until light and fluffy.
4. Stir half of the flour mixture into the batter, followed by the water. Now stir in the second half of the flour mixture, then fold the sauerkraut into the batter.
5. Distribute the batter evenly between the baking pans and bake in the preheated oven for 32–34 minutes, or until the cakes spring back when lightly touched.
6. Let cool in the baking pan for 10 minutes, then remove the cakes from the baking pans and place on a rack to cool completely.
7. To assemble, slice off the tops of the cakes to create a flat surface. Place the first cake on a plate. Spread generously with frosting. Place the second cake, cut side down, on top. Press down lightly. Cover the sides of the cake with a thin coating of frosting. Spread or pipe a thicker layer of frosting on top. Decorate with sprinkles or a dusting of gold powder, or leave as is.

Cake-ies This batter will make 16–18 cake-ies; preheat the oven as above and bake for 12–14 minutes. To freeze them, simply freeze mounds of batter on a plate, then wrap airtight and freeze for up to 6 months. Bake from frozen for 12–14 minutes.

Chill
The batter can be kept in the fridge in an airtight container for 3 days.

Freeze
Once completely cooled, wrap the unfrosted cakes airtight and freeze for up to 6 months.

Defrost
Let the cakes thaw in the fridge overnight or on the counter for a few hours, then assemble and frost.

QUIC

KIES

QUICKIES are at the heart of Batch Baking – make-ahead batters to make busy mornings easier. Having pancake batter ready to go in the fridge, or some scone or biscuit dough portions individually wrapped in the freezer, means you always have something ready to bake.

'I'D NO TIME TO WASTE. BREAKFAST, SCRUMPTIOUS, ON THE PLATE. SMILES ALL AROUND.'

ANONYMOUS, 21ST CENTURY BERLIN

AND JUST LIKE THAT...

Breakfast is one of life's simple pleasures, but despite – or perhaps due to – the technology of today, we seem to have less time than ever for it. Let's change that, dear reader. Meet my quick and easy morning ideas.

They say breakfast is the most important meal of the day. I love breakfast all day. Every day. Here is a chapter of waffles, pancakes, cake-ies and scones (biscuits) that are more delicious than anything in your wildest dreams. Forget boxed mixes and wannabe frozen goods – anything you make yourself will taste infinitely better.

How about a sweet potato waffle, delicious smothered in butter and dripping with maple syrup. Or just grab one off the plate and munch it on the way to work, school or the gym.

Pancakes anyone? In the 'old days' we had pancake mix in a box, ready to go. Guess what? You can make that batter yourself. Have it ready in the fridge and before you can say, 'did you finish your homework?', have the finest, most delectable warm pancakes on the table. Butter. Real maple syrup. Oh Canada!

And what about the biscuits? Not the cookie kind, but ones like *scones*. I've gone to the *wild side* with a potato chip and sour cream version. And I've also given you the best recipe for classic baking powder biscuits. Call them a scone, call them a biscuit, simply call them the most delicious thing you've made in a long time!

Just because you're short of time in a morning doesn't mean you have to miss out on freshly baked goodies. With these batters and doughs in your fridge or freezer, you'll have hot-out-of-the-oven treats any day of the week.

Waffle and pancake pointers
- invest in some reusable, airtight containers for the waffle and pancake batters
- the batters love to rest and hydrate in the fridge – take your time with them
- for light and airy pancakes, flip them only once

Tips for brilliant biscuits and scones
- for a light biscuit, sift the flour, cornflour (cornstarch), baking powder, salt and bicarbonate of soda (baking soda)
- turning and folding the dough creates layers of flaky dough and airiness
- for a nice golden colour, brush the biscuits with melted butter, cream or milk before baking
- the simpler the dough or batter, the quicker it oxidizes in the fridge

STRAWBERRY CORNFLAKE BREAKFAST CAKE-IES

I am not a big fan of eating breakfast, but by mid-morning I need *something*.
These cornflake cake-ies are perfect with a cup of coffee or a glass of juice.
Just the right thing to get me into the second half of the day!

MAKES 12-14

160g (scant 1¼ cups) plain (all-purpose) flour

1 tsp baking powder

½ tsp vanilla salt (see page 202) or salt

125g (1 stick) butter, softened

50g (¼ cup) caster (granulated) sugar

2 eggs

150ml (⅔ cup) whole milk

1 tsp vanilla extract (see page 202)

40g (¾ cup) cornflakes

20g (¾ cup loosely packed) freeze-dried strawberries or raspberries

1 x quantity Cornflake Streusel (see page 211)

1. Whisk together the flour, baking powder and vanilla salt or salt. Set aside.
2. In a large bowl, beat the butter with the sugar until creamy. Add the eggs and continue to beat until light and fluffy; about 1–2 minutes. Beat in the milk and vanilla extract, and stir in the cornflakes.
3. Using a spatula, fold in the flour mixture, followed by the freeze-dried berries. Do not overmix.
4. Transfer to an airtight container and refrigerate for at least 1 hour.
5. When ready to bake, preheat the oven to 180°C fan (350°F/Gas 4) and line a baking sheet with parchment.
6. The dough will be rather stiff. Using an ice cream scoop or a tablespoon, place mounds of the batter 5cm (2in) apart on the lined baking sheet. Press a tablespoon or more of streusel onto each cake-ie.
7. Bake in the preheated oven for about 13 minutes, or until the cake-ies are golden and spring back when touched. Transfer to a wire rack to cool.

Chill
The batter can be kept in the fridge in an airtight container for up to 4 days.

Freeze
Shape the cake-ies into mounds on a plate, press streusel onto them and freeze. Once frozen, wrap airtight and freeze for up to 6 months.

Bake from frozen
Preheat the oven as above and bake the cake-ies on a lined baking sheet for about 14–16 minutes, or until golden.

BLUEBERRY CORNBREAD CAKE-IES

These blueberry cornbread cake-ies are a *summer-state-of-mind*. You must use fresh, seasonal blueberries – and it's worth the wait.

MAKES 12-14

180g (1⅓ cups) plain (all-purpose) flour

100g (⅔ cup) coarse polenta (cornmeal) (do not use instant polenta)

2 tsp baking powder

½ tsp vanilla salt (see page 202) or salt

100g (6½ tbsp) butter

75g (⅓ cup) Demerara (raw) sugar

2 eggs

150ml (scant ⅔ cup) milk

1 tsp vanilla extract (see page 202)

200g (7oz/about 1 cup) blueberries, washed and dried

1. Whisk together the flour, polenta (cornmeal), baking powder and vanilla salt or salt. Set aside.
2. Melt the butter. While it is still hot, pour it into a mixing bowl and whisk in the sugar, followed by the eggs, milk and vanilla extract.
3. Stir in the flour mixture. Combine until the batter just barely comes together. Fold in the blueberries. Don't overmix or break up the berries.
4. Transfer the batter to an airtight container and refrigerate for at least 1 hour.
5. When ready to bake, preheat the oven to 200°C fan (400°F/Gas 6) and line a baking sheet with parchment.
6. The dough will be rather stiff. Using an ice cream scoop or a tablespoon, place mounds of the batter 5cm (2in) apart on the lined baking sheet.
7. Bake in the preheated oven for about 13 minutes, or until the cake-ies are golden and spring back when touched. Transfer to a wire rack to cool.

Tip These are nice topped with one of the sweet streusels (see page 211).

Chill
The batter can be kept in the fridge in an airtight container for 4 days.

Freeze
Simply freeze mounds of batter on a plate. Once frozen, wrap airtight and freeze for up to 6 months.

Bake from frozen
Preheat the oven as above and bake on a lined baking sheet for about 14 minutes, or until the cake-ies are golden and spring back when touched.

BANANA LEMON GRANOLA CAKE-IES

Of course you could simply skip making the cake-ies and only do the granola. But you can't make someone happy with 'a granola' nor can you grab 'a granola' and eat it on the way to I-don't-know-where. So take a moment, enjoy life and make the cake-ies... because the journey is as important as the destination. Pictured page 96.

MAKES 24

VEGAN

150g (1 cup plus 2 tbsp) plain (all-purpose) flour

75g (generous ⅓ cup) wholemeal (whole-wheat) flour

1 tsp baking powder

1 tsp bicarbonate of soda (baking soda)

½ tsp vanilla salt (see page 202) or salt

½ tsp ground cinnamon

¼ tsp ground nutmeg

75g (⅓ cup) Demerara (raw) sugar

2 ripe bananas, mashed or puréed (about 200g/7oz)

150ml (½ cup plus 2 tbsp) plant-based milk

grated zest and juice of 1 lemon

100ml (scant ½ cup) vegetable oil

150g (scant 1 cup) Homemade Granola (see page 213) or store-bought

1 apple, cored and coarsely grated (feel free to leave the peel on)

100g (¾ cup) pitted dates or other dried fruit, chopped

For topping (optional)

2 tbsp Demerara (raw) sugar

½ tsp ground cinnamon

1. In a large bowl combine the flours, baking powder, bicarbonate of soda (baking soda), vanilla salt or salt, spices and sugar. Set aside.
2. Whisk the puréed bananas with the milk, lemon zest and juice and oil.
3. Add the liquid ingredients to the flour mixture and stir just to combine. Add the granola, grated apple and dried fruit. Stir to barely combine. Do not overmix.
4. Transfer the batter to an airtight container and refrigerate for at least 2 hours.
5. When ready to bake, preheat the oven to 180°C fan (350°F/Gas 4) and line a baking sheet with parchment. Combine the sugar with the cinnamon, if using.
6. Using an ice cream scoop or a tablespoon, place mounds of batter 5cm (2in) apart on the lined baking sheet. Sprinkle with the sugar and cinnamon.
7. Bake in the preheated oven for 14 minutes, or until golden and the cake-ies spring back when lightly touched.

Chill
The batter can be kept in the fridge in an airtight container for up to 3 days.

Freeze
Simply freeze mounds of batter on a plate sprinkled with cinnamon and sugar. Once frozen, wrap airtight and freeze for up to 6 months.

Bake from frozen
Preheat the oven as above and bake on a lined baking sheet for 16–18 minutes, or until the cake-ies are golden.

BRAN-APPLE CAKE-IES

There was a famous 6-week bran muffin recipe my mother always spoke about. Though I do feel 6 weeks is a bit long to store a batter, I will take 6 months frozen. And to be perfectly honest, I'll take a fresh bran cake-ie any day! Pictured page 97.

MAKES 18

VEGAN

1 tbsp ground linseeds (flaxseeds)

3 tbsp hot water

250ml (1 cup) plant-based milk

1 tsp vinegar (I like to use apple cider vinegar)

50ml (3½ tbsp) vegetable oil

50ml (3½ tbsp) maple syrup

1 tsp vanilla extract (see page 202)

75g (1⅓ cups) bran

30g (⅓ cup) coarse oatmeal (steel-cut oats)

175g (1¼ cups) plain (all-purpose) flour

1 tbsp chia seeds

1 tsp bicarbonate of soda (baking soda)

2 tsp baking powder

½ tsp salt

¼–½ tsp ground cinnamon

75g (½ cup) dark brown muscovado sugar

1 apple, cored and coarsely grated (feel free to leave the peel on)

75g (½ cup) raisins or chopped dates

1. Begin by mixing the ground linseeds (flaxseeds) with the hot water. Let sit for about 10 minutes in the fridge until it becomes gelatinous.
2. Combine the plant-based milk with vinegar, vegetable oil, maple syrup and vanilla extract. Set aside. In a large bowl, combine the bran, oats, flour, chia seeds, bicarbonate of soda (baking soda), baking powder, salt, cinnamon and brown sugar. Mix well. Set aside.
3. Combine the grated apple or pear with the raisins or chopped dates. Set aside.
4. Add the linseed (flaxseed) mixture to the plant-based milk mixture and combine with the flour mixture. Stir to barely combine, then add the grated and dried fruit.
5. Transfer the batter to an airtight container and place in the fridge for at least 6 hours (to thicken).
6. When ready to bake, preheat the oven to 190°C fan (375°F/Gas 5) and line a baking sheet with parchment.
7. Using an ice cream scoop or a tablespoon, place mounds of batter onto the lined baking sheet, about 5cm (2in) apart.
8. Bake in the preheated oven for 13 minutes, or until browned and slightly puffy. Let cool on the baking sheet for 5 minutes, then transfer to a wire rack.

Chill
The batter can be stored in an airtight container in the fridge for up to 10 days.

Freeze
Simply freeze mounds of batter on a plate. Once frozen, wrap airtight and freeze for up to 6 months.

Bake from frozen
Preheat the oven as above and bake on a lined baking sheet for 15–17 minutes, or until browned and puffy.

MAPLE NUT CAKE-IES

Growing up in the States instilled in me a love for pecans, vanilla and maple syrup. These cake-ies are everything I want from this combo: sweet, nutty, slightly salty and dee-licious warm with butter! You can substitute walnuts for pecans, just make sure they're not the bitter kind. There is no substitute for maple syrup!

MAKES 20

250g (1¾ cups) plain (all-purpose) flour

100g (1 cup) coarse oatmeal (steel-cut oats)

75g (scant ½ cup) light soft brown sugar

2 tsp baking powder

½ tsp bicarbonate of soda (baking soda)

½ tsp salt

1 tsp ground cinnamon

¼ tsp nutmeg

200ml (¾ cup plus 1½ tbsp) buttermilk

50ml (3½ tbsp) maple syrup

1 egg

50g (3 tbsp plus 1 tsp) butter, melted

50g (scant ½ cup) pecan or walnut halves, coarsely chopped

50g (⅓ cup) pitted dates, chopped

20 pecan and walnut halves, to decorate (optional)

1. In a large bowl, combine the flour, oats, light soft brown sugar, baking powder, bicarbonate of soda (baking soda), salt and spices. Mix well. Set aside.
2. In a measuring jug (cup), whisk together the buttermilk, maple syrup, egg and melted butter. Set aside.
3. In a separate small bowl mix the chopped nuts and the dates. Set aside.
4. Add the buttermilk mixture to the flour mixture. Stir to barely combine, then add the chopped nuts and dates. Mix well, being careful not to overmix the batter.
5. Transfer the batter to an airtight container and refrigerate for at least 1 hour.
6. When ready to bake, preheat the oven to 180°C fan (350°F/Gas 4) and line a baking sheet with parchment.
7. Using an ice cream scoop or a tablespoon, place mounds of batter onto the lined baking sheet, about 5cm (2in) apart. If desired, place a pecan and walnut half on top of each cake-ie.
8. Bake in the preheated oven for about 15 minutes, or until browned and slightly puffy. Let cool on the baking sheet for 5 minutes, then transfer to a wire rack to cool completely.

Chill
The batter can be kept in the fridge in an airtight container for up to 5 days.

Freeze
Simply freeze mounds of batter on a plate. Once frozen, wrap airtight and freeze for up to 6 months.

Bake from frozen
Preheat the oven as above and bake the cake-ies on a lined baking sheet for about 15–16 minutes, or until browned.

CLASSIC BISCUITS

A fantastic biscuit is like a crisp, white shirt – it can be whatever you want it to be. Dress it up with a tasty spread or revel in its simplicity with nothing but a cup of tea. I've reduced this recipe to the max to give you a biscuit with a perfect, flaky texture devoid of any embellishment – not even sugar! Laminating the dough creates a croissant-like texture. Try these with the Honey Butter or Garlic Herb Butter (see page 214).

MAKES 8-10

350g (2⅔ cups) plain (all-purpose) flour, plus extra for dusting

4 tsp baking powder

1 tsp salt

125g (1 stick) butter, sliced and very cold

250ml (1 cup) whole milk, cold

25g (scant ¼ stick) butter, softened

1. Sift the flour, baking powder and salt into a mixing bowl. Work in the cold butter with your fingertips or a knife and fork until the mixture resembles little peas. Add the cold milk and stir just until the dough comes together. This dough is quite soft, so work quickly and do not over-knead.
2. Turn the dough out onto a lightly floured work surface. Quickly and lightly knead it together. Gently press the dough into a rectangle, about 1.5cm (⅝in) thick. Now we are going to laminate the dough. Spread half the softened butter on the upper two-thirds of the rectangle. Fold the bottom end of the dough into the centre, then the other end (with the butter) over it, like a letter. You will have three layers of dough. Turn the dough so the closed edge is on the right and quickly press the dough to a rectangle again, 1.5cm (⅝in) thick. Smear the rest of the softened butter on the upper two-thirds of the dough. Fold the bottom third to the centre and fold the top third over it like a letter.
3. Quickly shape the dough into a log, 22cm (8¾in) long and 6cm (2½in) in diameter. Wrap in parchment and refrigerate for at least 30 minutes.
4. When ready to bake, preheat the oven to 220°C fan (425°F/Gas 7) and line a baking sheet with parchment.
5. Slice the dough into biscuits, 2.5cm (1in) thick and place on the baking sheet.
6. Bake in the preheated oven for 12–13 minutes, or until golden.
7. Let the biscuits cool on the baking sheet for 10 minutes, then transfer to a wire rack to cool completely.

Chill
The dough can be kept wrapped in the fridge (either in a log or sliced) for up to 2 days.

Freeze
Simply freeze the sliced biscuit dough. Once frozen, wrap airtight and freeze for up to 6 months.

Bake from frozen
Preheat the oven as above and bake the biscuits on a lined baking sheet for about 13–14 minutes, or until golden.

POTATO SOUR CREAM BISCUITS WITH HERBS

One might think that an American biscuit is just a biscuit (what the British call a scone)… but to a baker, there is a whole *world* of biscuits out there. For me, this biscuit recipe, made with crisps (potato chips), is a deconstructed baked potato with sour cream, bacon and herbs. Smoked scamorza is a perfect substitution for bacon; it imparts that smoky flavour without the bacon-frying hassle!

MAKES 10-12

225g (1²/₃ cups) plain (all-purpose) flour, plus extra for dusting

100g (3½oz) finely ground crisps (potato chips) (I like the kind with vinegar!)

3 tsp baking powder

½ tsp bicarbonate of soda (baking soda)

¾ tsp sea salt

½ tsp caster (granulated) sugar

75g (²/₃ cup) coarsely grated smoked scamorza (or other smoked cheese)

2–3 tbsp roughly chopped herbs, such as tarragon, chives and thyme

freshly ground black pepper

125g (1 stick) butter, very cold, cut into thin slices

200g (scant 1 cup) sour cream, cold

2–3 tbsp cold milk or cold water

1. In a large bowl, whisk together the flour, ground crisps (potato chips), baking powder, bicarbonate of soda (baking soda), salt and sugar.

2. In a small bowl, combine the grated cheese, herbs and several grindings of black pepper. Blend in the cold butter with your fingertips until the mixture resembles coarse meal. Add the cold sour cream and the milk or water, as needed. Stir just until a dough comes together.

3. Place the dough onto a lightly floured work surface. Roll the dough into a log, about 24cm (9in) long and 5–6cm (2–2¼in) in diameter. Wrap in parchment and place in the fridge for at least 15 minutes.

4. When ready to bake, preheat the oven to 220°C fan (425°F/Gas 7) and line a baking sheet with parchment.

5. Slice 2.5cm (1in) slices from the log and place on the prepared baking sheet.

6. Bake in the preheated oven for about 15 minutes, or until golden. Let cool on the baking sheet for 10 minutes, then transfer to a wire rack to cool completely.

Chill
The dough can be kept in the fridge, wrapped airtight, for up to 2 days.

Freeze
Simply freeze the sliced biscuit dough. Once frozen, wrap airtight and freeze for up to 6 months.

Bake from frozen
Preheat the oven as above and bake the biscuits on a lined baking sheet for about 16–17 minutes, or until golden.

BUTTERMILK BISCUITS

I have lived in Europe longer than the States, but I have never lost my love for American biscuits, or scones as they are known in the UK. Which came first, the biscuit or the scone? Does it really matter as long as you have a light, buttery, airy piece of heaven!

MAKES 12

250g (1¾ cups) plain (all-purpose) flour, plus extra for dusting

75g (⅔ cup) cornflour (cornstarch)

2½ tsp baking powder

1 tsp bicarbonate of soda (baking soda)

1–3 tsp caster (granulated) sugar, to taste

1 tsp salt

150g (1¼ sticks) butter, thinly sliced and chilled in the freezer

200ml (¾ cup plus 1½ tbsp) buttermilk, cold

30g (2 tbsp) butter, softened

1. Sift together the flour, cornflour (cornstarch), baking powder, bicarbonate of soda (baking soda), sugar and salt. Blend in the cold butter with your fingertips or a knife and fork until the mixture resembles coarse meal. Add the cold buttermilk and stir just until the dough comes together.

2. Turn the dough out onto a lightly floured work surface. Quickly and *lightly* knead it together. Roll out the dough into a rectangle, about 6mm (¼in) thick. Spread half the softened butter in a thin layer on the upper two-thirds of the dough. Fold the bottom end of the dough into the centre, then the other end (with the butter) over it, like a letter. You will have three layers of dough. Turn the dough so the closed edge is on the right and repeat: roll out the dough to a rectangle, smear the rest of the softened butter on the upper two-thirds of the dough, fold the bottom third to the centre and fold the top third over it like a letter.

3. Wrap in parchment and refrigerate for at least 45 minutes.

4. When ready to bake, preheat the oven to 220°C fan (425°F/Gas 7) and line a baking sheet with parchment.

5. Roll out the dough on a lightly floured work surface to 2cm (¾in) thickness. Use a glass or a 7.5cm (3in) cookie cutter dipped in flour to cut it into portions and place on the baking sheet. Cut the biscuits very close together so you don't have to re-roll the dough, which can over-work the gluten and make a tough biscuit!

6. Bake in the preheated oven for about 11–12 minutes, or until golden. Let cool on the baking sheet for 10 minutes, then transfer to a wire rack to cool completely.

Chill

The dough can be kept in the fridge, wrapped airtight, for up to 48 hours.

Freeze

Simply freeze the cut biscuit dough. Once frozen, wrap airtight and freeze for up to 6 months.

Bake from frozen

Preheat the oven as above and bake the biscuits on a lined baking sheet for about 12–13 minutes, or until golden.

SPICED FRUIT AND NUT SCONES

Ok, so these scones are a bit busy. Think of them as a symphony for your palate – the warmth of the spices, the delicate flaky texture, the surprising flavour of dried pears.

MAKES 8

300g (2¼ cups) plain (all-purpose) flour

50g (¼ cup) Demerara (raw) sugar

3 tsp baking powder

¾ tsp bicarbonate of soda (baking soda)

½ tsp vanilla salt (see page 202) or salt

1 tsp ground turmeric

50g (1¾oz) crystallized ginger, finely chopped

100g (3½oz) dried pears or dried apricots, coarsely chopped

100g (1 cup) flaked (sliced) almonds or chopped pecans

150ml (½ cup plus 2 tbsp) double (heavy) cream, cold

1 egg

125g (1 stick) butter, cut up and cold

For topping

2 tbsp Demerara (raw) sugar

¼ tsp ground cinnamon

¼ tsp ground turmeric

1. In a large bowl combine the flour, sugar, baking powder, bicarbonate of soda (baking soda), vanilla salt or salt, turmeric and crystallized ginger. Set aside.
2. In a small bowl combine the dried fruit with the nuts. Set aside.
3. Whisk together the cold cream and egg. Set aside.
4. Combine the sugar and spices for topping. Set aside.
5. Blend the cold butter into the flour mixture with your fingertips or a pastry blender until the mixture resembles coarse meal. Stir in the cold cream and egg just until a dough forms. Add the dried fruit and nuts. Knead the dough on a lightly floured surface just until it comes together. Don't overwork the dough.
6. When ready to bake, preheat the oven to 195°C fan (380°F/Gas 5) and line a baking sheet with parchment.
7. Shape the dough into a 20cm (8in) disc. Cut it into quarters, then cut each quarter in half again; giving you 8 'slices'. You can also pat the dough to about 2cm (¾in) thickness and use a glass or a cookie cutter dipped in flour to cut the dough into 8 portions. Cut them close together and don't re-roll out the dough.
8. Arrange the scones on the baking sheet. Sprinkle with the sugar/spice mixture.
9. Bake in the preheated oven for 15–16 minutes, or until golden. Let cool on the baking sheet for 10 minutes, then transfer to a wire rack to cool completely.

Chill
The dough portions can be kept in the fridge, wrapped airtight, for up to 48 hours.

Freeze
Simply freeze the cut scone dough. Once frozen, wrap airtight and freeze for up to 6 months.

Bake from frozen
Preheat the oven as above and bake on a lined baking sheet for 16–17 minutes until golden.

OATMEAL BISCUITS WITH FREEZE-DRIED BERRIES AND DATES

These biscuits are simply delicious. As with all biscuits and scones, it's all about the ingredients' temperatures. Liquids and margarine must be super cold for a light and flaky result. Keep any kneading to an absolute minimum.

MAKES 8

VEGAN

280g (2 cups) plain (all-purpose) flour, plus extra for dusting

100g (1 cup) coarse oatmeal (steel-cut oats) or jumbo rolled (old-fashioned) oats

50–75g (⅓–½ cup) light soft brown sugar, to taste

3 tsp baking powder

½ tsp bicarbonate of soda (baking soda)

½ tsp ground nutmeg

½ tsp salt

100ml (scant ½ cup) plant-based milk, cold, plus extra for brushing

1 tsp any vinegar

2 tbsp maple syrup

125g (4oz) vegan margarine, very cold, cut into thinnish slices

10g (⅓ cup loosely packed) freeze-dried berries

100g (¾ cup) pitted dates or dried figs, chopped

1. In a large bowl combine the flour, oats, sugar, baking powder, bicarbonate of soda (baking soda), nutmeg and salt. Set aside. In a measuring jug (cup), combine the cold plant-based milk, vinegar and maple syrup. Set aside.

2. Blend the margarine into the flour mixture with your fingertips or a pastry blender until the mixture resembles coarse meal. Add the cold plant-based milk mixture and stir just until a dough forms. Add the freeze-dried berries and dried fruit. Knead the dough on a lightly floured surface just until it comes together.

3. Shape the dough into a disc, about 20cm (8in) diameter and cut the circle into eight wedges. Alternatively, pat the dough to about 2cm (¾in) thickness and use a glass or a cookie cutter dipped in flour to cut the dough into 8 circles. Cut the biscuits very close together, so you don't have to re-roll out the dough, which can over-work the gluten and make a tough biscuit! You should end up with 8 pieces.

4. When ready to bake, preheat the oven to 200°C fan (400°F/Gas 6) and line a baking sheet with parchment.

5. Arrange the biscuits on the baking sheet and brush with plant-based milk.

6. Bake in the preheated oven for 15–16 minutes, or until golden. Let cool on the baking sheet for 10 minutes, then transfer to a wire rack to cool completely.

Chill
The dough shapes can be stored in the fridge, wrapped airtight, for up to 3 days.

Freeze
Simply freeze the cut biscuit dough. Once frozen, wrap airtight and freeze for up to 6 months.

Bake from frozen
Preheat the oven as above and bake on a lined baking sheet for about 16–17 minutes.

SOUR CREAM PANCAKES

This recipe offers flexibility. The base recipe can be combined with your choice of oats, polenta (cornmeal) or whole-grain flour. Fry them or make sheetpan pancakes.

MAKES ABOUT 15

2 eggs

200g (generous ¾ cup) sour cream

200ml (¾ cup plus 1½ tbsp) whole milk

75g (generous ½ cup) whole-grain flour or 75g (½ cup) polenta (cornmeal) (do not use instant polenta) or 75g (¾ cup) porridge oats

300g (scant 2¼ cups) plain (all-purpose) flour

2 tsp baking powder

1 tsp bicarbonate of soda (baking soda)

¼ tsp active dried yeast

¾ tsp salt

1–2 tbsp caster (granulated) sugar

75g (5 tbsp) butter, melted and slightly cooled

butter and vegetable oil, for frying

fresh or frozen berries, or sliced fruit (optional)

Note This makes a very thick and airy batter that continues to thicken with time. If you prefer a thinner, batter, add a total of 300ml (1¼ cups) milk.

1. Combine the eggs with sour cream and milk. Set aside.
2. In a large bowl, combine your choice of grain with the flour, baking powder, bicarbonate of soda (baking soda), yeast, salt and sugar. Add the egg mixture. Stir to combine. Do not overmix. Mix in the melted butter.
3. Transfer the batter to an airtight container or place cling film (plastic wrap) on the surface to prevent it from oxidizing. Let rest in the fridge for at least 6 hours.
4. To cook, heat a griddle (grill pan) or frying pan until a few drops of water sizzle. Melt 1 tbsp butter and a bit of vegetable oil. Using a large spoon, ladle or ice cream scoop, place some batter onto the griddle. To add any sliced fruit or berries, simply press lightly onto the surface of the batter.
5. Cook over a medium heat until the surface is sprinkled with large bubbles, about 4 minutes, then turn and cook until the other side is lightly browned.

Sheetpan pancakes Preheat the oven to 230°C fan (450°F/Gas 8). Lightly brush a baking sheet with melted butter, line with parchment, then brush the parchment with more melted butter. Spread the batter over the parchment and press sliced fruits or chopped chocolate over the surface. Bake for 12 minutes, then remove from the oven and brush with melted butter. Preheat a grill (broiler) to high and grill (broil) the sheetpan pancakes for 2 minutes. Slice and serve! Pictured page 112–113.

Chill
The batter can be kept in the fridge in an airtight container for 3 days.

Freeze
Open freeze the cooled, cooked pancakes. Once frozen, wrap airtight and freeze for up to 3 months.

Defrost
Simply thaw in the toaster when ready to eat.

SWEET POTATO WAFFLES

What can I say? Sweet potatoes are one of those chameleon vegetables that morph into so many different flavours and textures depending upon how you cook them and with which ingredients they're combined. Maple-y with a fluffy texture, just grab one of these waffles on-the-go, you don't even need a napkin!

MAKES 6

VEGAN

250g (9oz/about 2 small) sweet potatoes

400ml (1⅔ cups) plant-based milk

2 tsp cider vinegar

75ml (⅓ cup) vegetable oil

275g (2 cups) plain (all-purpose) flour

1 tbsp baking powder

1 tsp bicarbonate of soda (baking soda)

¾ tsp vanilla salt (see page 202) or salt

3 tbsp dark or light soft brown sugar

¼ tsp grated nutmeg

½ tsp ground cinnamon

To serve

raspberries and maple syrup or ground cinnamon and sugar (optional)

1. Peel and boil the sweet potatoes or roast them whole and scoop out the flesh. Purée and let cool, then weigh out 250g (9oz).
2. Whisk together the plant-based milk, vinegar and vegetable oil. Whisk in the sweet potato purée and set aside.
3. In a large bowl combine the flour, baking powder, bicarbonate of soda (baking soda), vanilla salt or salt, sugar and spices.
4. Add the liquids to the flour mixture and stir to barely combine.
5. When ready to make waffles, preheat the waffle iron and cook the waffle mixture according to manufacturer's instructions. Serve with raspberries and maple syrup, a sprinkling of cinnamon and sugar, or simply plain.

Tip To keep the waffles warm before eating, put them on a plate or rack in a single layer in a barely warm oven and cover them lightly with a dish towel. This way, the waffles will neither dry out nor steam each other!

Chill
The batter can be stored in an airtight container in the fridge for up to 4 days.

Freeze
Open freeze the cooled, cooked waffles. Once frozen, wrap airtight and freeze for up to 6 months.

Defrost
Simply thaw in the toaster when ready to eat.

SOURD

OUGH

SOURDOUGH is a thing of

beauty, and there has been a lot written about it.
Maybe one day, I will also write a treatise on
sourdough starter. Until then, think of this chapter as
your CliffsNotes. The quick set-up instructions for
those of you who want to hit the ground running.

LIFE'S TOO SHORT TO BUY BAD BREAD

BAKING WITHOUT YEAST ON A SNOWY EVENING

What dough this is I think I know
Some folks they call it sourdough
A dough where yeast you do not need
The microbes on their own do grow

Of course we must a great deal knead
And don't forget the dough to feed
The starter lasts for years to come
Cuz crusty bread's a thing we need

So please my friends, don't look so glum
The sourdough starter ain't so dumb
Bacteria builds from water and wheat
Resulting in an open crumb

So set the oven to preheat
So much to bake before we eat
So much to bake before we eat
Homage to Robert Frost.

Harnessing wild yeast

Many years ago, someone gave me some sourdough starter together with a long, complicated list of its feeding schedule. I was sure I was gonna kill it. Like a self-fulfilling prophecy, it bubbled up and died. Since then, I have realized two things: I am not a murderer, and a sourdough starter is fun and easy.

When you create sourdough starter, you harness the wild yeast and bacteria that exist in the air and in the flour. Sourdough is *alive*. A dough or batter made with sourdough needs more time than one made with active dried yeast. It can maintain in the fridge much longer, slowly developing a rich flavour and texture. It will not double in bulk during rising.

Sourdough means more than just loaves. When you have your sourdough starter, you can whip up buns, pizza dough, pancakes and waffles.

Tip You can substitute 100g (⅓ cup) starter for 6g (scant ¼oz) active dried yeast. To use sourdough starter instead of dried yeast, reduce the volume of liquids by the volume of the starter (add a bit of water if needed). To use active dried yeast instead of sourdough starter, substitute the starter for the same volume of water.

SOURDOUGH STARTER

To make a sourdough starter, we begin with two ingredients: pineapple juice and flour. Pineapple juice regulates the pH of the initial starter and inhibits the growth of bad bacteria. It has the right acidity to keep the starter happy and promotes good bacterial growth.

Choose a container made of plastic, glass or ceramic. Make sure it's big enough for at least 1 litre/quart of starter and has a lid. You can also fashion a lid made of paper towel and a rubber band, which lets the mixture breathe. Have all ingredients at room temperature.

MAKES ABOUT 300G (1 CUP)

Day 1

Mix together the following and then cover:

4 tbsp plain (all-purpose) or strong white bread flour

4 tbsp unsweetened pineapple juice

Day 2

Stir in the following and then cover:

4 tbsp plain (all-purpose) or strong white bread flour

4 tbsp unsweetened pineapple juice

Day 3 and day 4

Stir in the following and then cover:

4 tbsp plain (all-purpose) or strong white bread flour

4 tbsp water

Day 5

Divide the sourdough in half. Discard half (or give it to a neighbour or someone you'd like to meet). Then stir in:

4 tbsp plain (all-purpose) or strong white bread flour

4 tbsp water

Why discard half the starter? This reduces the starter volume, allowing half the yeast to be fed twice as much.

Now what? If you want to bake often with it, keep the starter on your kitchen counter (18–20°C/64–68°F). Once a week, discard half the starter or use it in a recipe and stir in 100ml (scant ½ cup) water and 100g (⅔ cup) flour. If you want the starter to *sleep* because you're too busy to bake, simply place it in the fridge. The day before you want to use it, discard half the starter and feed it with 100ml (scant ½ cup) water and 100g (⅔ cup) flour. Let rest, covered on your kitchen counter. The next day it will be bubbly and ready to go. This is known as a 'fed starter'.

Troubleshooting If the starter separates and has a brownish liquid on top (known as *the hooch*) it means it's tired and has fermented. The starter developed faster than you could use it. No problem. Simply stir everything together, weigh out 100g (3½oz) starter and add 100ml (scant ½ cup) water and 100g (⅔ cup) flour. Feed it with 100ml (scant ½ cup) water and 100g (⅔ cup) flour every day for 2–3 days and you'll be back on track.

SOURDOUGH PANCAKES

Anything made with sourdough has a special depth of flavour and these pancakes are no exception. Thick, fluffy, tangy and barely sweet, they're satisfying without being too filling. Make the batter the night before and they will be ready to cook for breakfast the next morning (and the morning after that) – perfect.

MAKES 25

2 eggs

500ml (2 cups) buttermilk

200g (½ cup plus 2 tbsp) sourdough starter, fed (see page 120)

450g (3⅓ cups) plain (all-purpose) flour

1 tsp baking powder

1½ tsp bicarbonate of soda (baking soda)

1 tsp salt

1 tbsp caster (granulated) sugar

50g (3 tbsp plus 1 tsp) butter, melted

sliced pear, sliced banana or a handful of blueberries (optional, but delicious!)

butter and vegetable oil, for frying

1. Combine the eggs with the buttermilk and sourdough starter. Set aside.
2. In a large bowl, combine the flour, baking powder, bicarbonate of soda (baking soda), salt and sugar. Add the egg mixture to the flour mixture. Stir to combine. Do not overmix. Gently mix in the melted butter.
3. Transfer the batter to an airtight container. Place a piece of cling film (plastic wrap) directly on top of the batter to prevent it from oxidizing. Allow to rest in the fridge for at least 6 hours.
4. When you are ready to cook, heat a griddle (grill) pan or frying pan (skillet) until a few drops of water sizzle. Melt a tablespoon of butter and a bit of vegetable oil. Using a large spoon, ladle or ice cream scoop, place some batter onto the griddle to form a 10–12.5cm (4–5in) pancake. If you want to add any sliced fruit or berries, now's the time. Simply press them lightly onto the surface of the batter.
5. Cook until the surface of the pancake is sprinkled with large bubbles, then turn and cook until the other side is lightly browned. Don't flip the pancakes from side to side, as this makes them lose their light texture.

Serving idea Serve with butter and maple syrup, honey or a fruit coulis.

Chill

The batter can be stored in an airtight container, with the surface covered in cling film (plastic wrap), in the fridge for up to 4 days.

Freeze

Open freeze the cooled, cooked pancakes. Once frozen, transfer to an airtight bag and freeze for up to 6 months.

Defrost

Simply thaw in the toaster when ready to eat.

APPLE AND CINNAMON WAFFLES

I am crazy about these waffles. These are plant-based with a subtle apple saucey, cinnamony, oaty flavour – what a way to start your day! A lot happens to this batter in the fridge: the sourdough rests; the oats get nice and soft; and the cinnamon marries with the apple sauce. Basically, all the actors come together. And you? All you have to do is enjoy the result!

MAKES 6

VEGAN

125ml (½ cup) water

125g (scant ⅓ cup) sourdough starter, fed (see page 120)

300ml (1¼ cups) unsweetened plant-based milk (I like to use oat milk or pea protein milk)

125g (½ cup) unsweetened apple sauce

50ml (3½ tbsp) vegetable oil (you can also use a nut oil or a fruity olive oil)

275g (2 cups) plain (all-purpose) flour

75g (¾ cup) fine or porridge oats

1 tbsp Demerara (raw) sugar

¾ tsp salt

¼ tsp bicarbonate of soda (baking soda)

¼ tsp ground cinnamon

1. Whisk together the water, sourdough starter, plant-based milk, apple sauce and vegetable oil. Set aside.
2. In a large bowl combine the flour, oats, sugar, salt, bicarbonate of soda (baking soda) and ground cinnamon.
3. Add the sourdough starter mixture to the flour mixture and stir to barely combine. Do not overwork the batter.
4. Transfer to an airtight container and refrigerate for at least 6 hours.
5. When ready to make waffles, heat the waffle iron according to the manufacturer's instructions. Bake the waffles until no more steam escapes from the waffle iron.

Serving idea Serve warm with maple syrup or apple sauce. I also like them with almond butter.

Tip To keep the waffles warm before eating, put them on a plate or rack in a single layer in a barely warm oven and cover them lightly with a dish towel. This way, the waffles will neither dry out nor steam each other.

Chill
The batter can be stored in an airtight container in the fridge for up to 3 days.

Freeze
Open freeze the cooled, cooked waffles. Once frozen, wrap airtight and freeze for up to 6 months.

Defrost
Simply thaw in the toaster when ready to eat.

SOURDOUGH PIZZA

Some people like their pizza crust very thin and some love a deep-dish pie. Well, this sourdough pizza dough is right in between; airy without being bready, completely supports every kind of topping, and is deliciously satisfying. It is an easy-going dough that will wait up to 5 days in the fridge for you to use it.

MAKES 3 PIZZAS

VEGAN

300ml (1¼ cups) cool water

200g (½ cup plus 2 tbsp) sourdough starter, fed (see page 120)

500g (generous 3½ cups) strong white bread flour

50g (generous ⅓ cup) whole-grain or rye flour

17g (1 tbsp) salt

olive oil, for greasing

polenta (cornmeal) or semolina, for dusting

Toppings

grated Parmesan cheese or vegan cheese

1 x quantity Simple Tomato Sauce (see page 215)

toppings of your choice

1. Combine the water with the sourdough starter and set aside. Combine the bread flour with the whole-grain or rye flour and salt. Stir the water and sourdough into the flour mixture and combine well. No need to knead the dough!

2. Place a few drops of olive oil into a bowl and roll the dough around in it. Place an airtight cover over the bowl and set in the fridge for at least 12 hours.

3. Several hours before baking, remove the amount of dough you need (200–300g/ ¾–1¼ cups per pizza) from the fridge. With the help of a bench scraper and a dusting of flour, roll each portion into a smooth ball. Place a kitchen towel lightly over the ball(s) and let sit for 2–3 hours until the dough has doubled in bulk.

4. 1 hour before baking, preheat the oven with your baking sheet or baking stone to 235°C fan (455°F/Gas 8).

5. Sprinkle a wooden baking paddle (peel) or the back of a baking sheet generously with polenta (cornmeal) or semolina to prevent the dough from sticking. Press the dough into a flat circle, moving and rotating, making sure it isn't sticking to the paddle.

6. Spread a few teaspoons of olive oil evenly on the dough and top with a small handful of finely grated cheese. Top with tomato sauce. Working quickly, finish off with your favourite toppings and some more grated cheese. Quickly, with the help of an offset spatula, transfer the pizza onto the heated surface. Bake in the preheated oven for 10–13 minutes, or until golden and the cheese is bubbling!

Chill

The dough can be stored in the fridge, covered airtight, for up to 5 days.

Freeze

Freeze portions of the dough in an airtight container for 6 months.

Defrost

Let the frozen dough thaw completely, then proceed with the recipe.

SOURDOUGH FLATBREADS

Think of this flatbread as a culinary cushion. The perfect pillow for the toppings of your dreams. The sky's the limit – your wishes and fantasies know no bounds here! Run with it, go with it, try new combinations and surprise yourself. No oven needed!

MAKES 8

150g (⅓ cup) sourdough starter, fed (see page 120)

250ml (1 cup) water

100g (scant ½ cup) yogurt

350g (2⅔ cups) plain (all-purpose) flour, plus extra for dusting

150g (1½ cups) rye flour

1 tsp Demerara (raw) sugar

1½ tsp salt

olive oil, for greasing

butter, for frying

1. Combine the sourdough starter with the water and yogurt.
2. In the bowl of a stand mixer fitted with a dough hook, combine the flours, sugar and salt. Add the liquids and mix for 3–4 minutes. The dough will be very soft and supple.
3. Add a few drops of olive oil to a clean bowl, roll the dough in it and cover airtight. Let it hydrate and rise in the bowl on your kitchen counter for 2 hours. Alternatively, if you'd like to use the dough later, place it in the fridge, covered airtight, for at least 8 hours.
4. When ready to use, prepare some toppings (see below). Heat some olive oil and a bit of butter in a heavy frying pan (skillet) over medium heat. Break off a piece of dough – as big or small as you please. The dough will be soft and a bit sticky. Combat the stickiness by using a bit of oil on your fingers. Flatten out the dough on your work surface to 1.5cm (½in) thick and place in the frying pan. Cook for about 4 minutes on each side. Finish with your toppings.

Favourite toppings
- thinly sliced pickled beetroot (beets) with soft goat's cheese, ricotta cheese and dill
- sautéed mushrooms with finely chopped onions, herbs and grated Manchego cheese
- skyr or sour cream, lox, red onions and sun-dried tomatoes
- Slow-roasted Tomatoes (see page 216), grated cheese and fresh herbs
- any kind of roasted vegetables combined with cheese or yogurt

Chill

The dough can be kept in the fridge in an airtight container for up to 5 days.

Freeze

Freeze portions of the dough in an airtight container for 6 months.

Defrost

Let the dough thaw completely in the fridge then proceed from step 4.

SOURDOUGH

SOURDOUGH MISO BREADS

If there was a snowstorm, and all I had were these little breads, a bit of flaky sea salt, some olive oil and a glass of water, I'd be at peace.

MAKES 10

VEGAN

500g (generous 3½ cups) strong white bread flour, plus extra for dusting

1¼ tsp salt

250ml (1 cup) water, room temperature

40g (2 tbsp) light miso

125g (scant ⅓ cup) sourdough starter, fed (see page 120)

2 tbsp olive oil, plus extra for greasing

1. In a large bowl, combine the bread flour with the salt and set aside.
2. Combine the water with miso and sourdough starter, then add this mixture to the flour.
3. Using a stand mixer fitted with a dough hook, knead the mixture for about 4 minutes until the dough is soft and supple (or knead by hand on a lightly floured surface). Put a few drops of olive oil in a bowl, swirl the dough in it and cover airtight.
4. Let the dough rest at room temperature for 5–6 hours before refrigerating for at least 12 hours.
5. When ready to bake, line a baking sheet with parchment. Pull off 100g (3½oz) portions of dough, as many as you want to bake right now, and roll and stretch each portion to a 30cm (12in) long thin breadstick/mini-baguette. Place on the lined baking sheet, dust with flour, cover and leave to rise for 6–8 hours. I like to place four glasses onto the baking sheet and cover the baking sheet with a large, plastic bag. The glasses prevent the bag from sticking to the bread. The rest of the dough can stay covered in the fridge for 5 days; simply tear off portions each day for fresh breads.
6. When ready to bake, preheat the oven to 220°C fan (425°F/Gas 7) and set a little ovenproof bowl filled with hot water on the floor of the oven.
7. Lightly flour then slash the surface of the little breads with a very sharp knife. Bake in the preheated oven for 15–17 minutes until golden.

Chill
The dough can be kept in the fridge, covered airtight, for up to 5 days.

Freeze
I do not recommend freezing this dough.

SOURDOUGH BURGER BUNS

Around the start of the pandemic, my family and I established a new tradition: Saturday burger night. I got my hands on some plant-based burgers (didn't tell the kids!), made some buns and it was a perfect moment. So perfect, that my husband wanted burgers the next night, too. "Nope", I said, "it's only special if it's one night a week". And so, years later, we are still enjoying our burger night – especially because the buns are just so good!

MAKES 14

650g (4²/₃ cups) plain (all-purpose) flour

1 tsp active dried yeast

1 tsp caster (granulated) sugar

2 tsp salt

1 tsp bicarbonate of soda (baking soda)

250g (¾ cup) sourdough starter, fed (see page 120)

200ml (¾ cup plus 1½ tbsp) water, room temperature

1 egg

300g (10½oz) potatoes, peeled, boiled, mashed and cooled

75g (5 tbsp) butter, softened and cut into chunks

For glazing

1 egg, beaten

4 tbsp mixed seeds

1. In a large bowl, combine the flour, yeast, sugar, salt and bicarbonate of soda (baking soda). Set aside.
2. In a large measuring jug (cup), combine the sourdough starter, water and the egg.
3. Add the liquids, the mashed potatoes and the chunks of butter to the flour mixture. Using a stand mixer fitted with a dough hook, knead the dough for 2–3 minutes (or knead by hand on a lightly floured surface). Be patient. This dough is a bit soft, but don't be tempted to add more flour.
4. Return the dough to the mixing bowl and cover airtight.
5. To bake on the same day, put the bowl in a warm place to rise until doubled in bulk, about 2 hours.
6. When ready to bake, line 2 baking sheets with parchment. Divide the dough into 14 portions, about 110g (3¾oz) each. Shape them into rounds, place on the baking sheet and brush with the beaten egg. Let rise for 30–45 minutes.
7. Preheat the oven to 200°C fan (400°F/Gas 6).
8. Right before baking, brush the surface of each bun again with the egg and sprinkle with some seeds. You can simply leave plain, if you prefer. Bake in the preheated oven for 13–15 minutes, or until golden.

Chill
The dough can be kept in the fridge, covered airtight, for up to 3 days. Continue with step 6.

Freeze
This dough doesn't freeze well, but you can freeze the baked buns. Let cool, cut in half, wrap airtight and freeze for 6 months.

Defrost
Let thaw in the fridge overnight or for a few hours on your counter, or pop them in your toaster.

BRE

BREAD is rewarding, visceral, elementary. Flour. Water. Salt. Yeast. The building blocks of the baking universe. The alpha and the omega. Humans have been baking bread for over 10,000 years, since a pivotal point in our history when we became settled, began farming and began baking. A wise person once told me, 'If a culture has no bread, it has no cuisine.'

LIKE ANY RELATIONSHIP, BAKING BREAD REQUIRES LOVE, PATIENCE AND UNDERSTANDING

BREAD EQUALS LIFE

Baking bread is a two-way street. Like any relationship, baking bread requires love, patience and understanding. There is an empathetic aspect to yeast, a quid-pro-quo. Give a dough the time it needs, and it will reward you with nourishment and a smell from your kitchen that hasn't changed in millennia.

The foundation of bread consists of four ingredients. The varying relation of them to one another will give you pizza, a crusty loaf, or a bread to celebrate a day of rest. Fill it, twist it, glaze it. Add some mashed potatoes, beetroot (beets), or some honey and lemon zest... wow. And when you're ready to advance, add some eggs and laminate the dough with butter for an irresistible Danish you'll be proud to call your own.

Fresh versus dried yeast

I love the spontaneity of dried yeast. It doesn't need to be proved and can simply be added directly to the flour. Dried yeast is also less temperature sensitive than fresh yeast, thus harder to *kill*.

If you make yeast dough often, you may prefer to get hold of fresh yeast. Prove it for a few minutes with whichever liquids are in the recipe to make sure the yeast is alive and active. Make sure the liquids are *bath temperature*. If after 5 minutes you see some little bubbles, you're good to continue with the recipe. If the mixture remains flat, get some new yeast and start again!

Working with dough

Letting the dough rise develops its flavour and texture. A cold, slow rise in the fridge (for days!) affords you the luxury of time. For quicker gratification and a test in patience, let it rise at room temperature. Never let the dough sit directly on top of a heater, you might kill the yeast. Like your grandmother, yeast does not like to be rushed.

A soft dough can be challenging to work with, but will give you amazing breads and crusts. Do not try to knead these doughs by hand and use as little flour as possible when handling. Remember: dough sticks to dough. A bench scraper is a lifesaver with wet doughs, as is working with a little bit of oil on your hands.

Freeze

Freeze a bread dough after the first rise, either in a loaf pan or simply in an airtight container. Let thaw overnight in the fridge or on your counter for several hours. Shape, give it a last 30-minute rise, then bake.

To freeze baked rolls or bread, wait until thoroughly cooled, then wrap airtight. Thaw for several hours on your kitchen counter or in a 140°C fan (275°F/Gas 1) oven until warmed though. You can freeze sliced bread. Simply pop in the toaster to thaw.

MY FAVE DAILY BREAD

Necessity is the mother of invention. When I decided that my café could bake better bread than we could buy, I had to first develop that recipe for my pastry chefs. Little known fact: most pastry chefs despise baking bread! Et voilà – my answer for people who don't like to bake bread, don't have any time and are maybe even a bit afraid of yeast!

MAKES 2 LOAVES

VEGAN

1kg (7¼ cups) strong white bread flour, plus extra for dusting (plain/all-purpose flour is also ok at a pinch)

7g sachet (¼oz envelope/ 2 tsp) active dried yeast
19g (3¼ tsp) salt
700ml (scant 3 cups) water
semolina, for dusting

1. Combine the flour with the yeast and salt. Add the water and knead with a stand mixer fitted with a dough hook for 1–2 minutes, but no longer.
2. Place the dough in an airtight container in the fridge and let rise overnight.
3. 2 hours before baking your bread, line a shallow bowl, approximately the size of loaf you'd like, with a dry kitchen towel and sprinkle generously with flour.
4. Remove a chunk of dough from the fridge. It will be cold and quite soft. Do not try to knead the dough. On a very lightly floured surface, gently flatten the dough, pull the sides up to the middle and pinch together to form a ball. Place this ball, seam-side up, into the prepared bowl. Cover with a dry kitchen towel and let rise at room temperature for 1½–2 hours.
5. 45 minutes prior to baking, place a baking sheet on a rack in the oven. Place a small heatproof bowl filled with water on the bottom of the oven and preheat the oven to 235°C fan (455°F/Gas 8) for at least 45 minutes. The intense heating of the baking sheet together with the humidity from the bowl of water aid in creating a perfect, crusty bread.
6. Remove the heated baking sheet from the oven. Sprinkle with semolina and plop the dough out of the bowl directly onto the baking sheet. With a sharp knife, slash the surface of the bread or simply leave the bread to split while baking.
7. Return the hot baking sheet to the oven and bake for about 30–35 minutes, or until the bread is golden and sounds hollow when the underside is tapped. Let cool on a wire rack.

Chill
The dough can be kept in the fridge in an airtight, container for up to 4 days.

Freeze
Divide the dough into portions and freeze in airtight containers for up to 6 months.

Defrost
Let the dough thaw overnight (or for at least 5 hours) in the fridge. Proceed from step 4.

CLASSIC PIZZA DOUGH

I've been baking pizza for years. I have concluded: the simpler the dough, the better. No pinch of sugar, no olive oil. Use 00 flour if you can find it – a very finely ground wheat flour. If you don't have it, simply use plain (all-purpose) flour plus a tablespoon of cornflour (cornstarch). This dough makes a thin-crust pizza. For a thicker one, try the Sourdough Pizza Dough, page 126.

MAKES 3 PIZZAS

VEGAN

1kg (7¼ cups) 00 flour, plus extra for dusting

20g (1 heaped tbsp) salt

7g sachet (¼oz envelope/ 2 tsp) active dried yeast

650ml (2¾ cups) water, room temperature

olive oil, for greasing

polenta (cornmeal) or semolina, for dusting the baking sheet

toppings of your choice (here I made a white pizza with Parmesan, mozzarella, ricotta and some blue cheese, but you could use tomato sauce and cheese or vegan cheese)

1. Combine the flour with the salt and yeast.
2. Stir in the water and combine well. Using a stand mixer fitted with a dough hook, knead the dough for a few minutes until it comes together. The dough is extremely soft. Use a scraper to handle it and don't try to knead it by hand.
3. Place a few drops of olive oil into a bowl, roll the dough around in it and cover airtight. For pizza now, let the dough rise at room temperature for 2–3 hours.
4. When ready to bake, remove some dough (200–300g/7–10½oz per pizza) and, with the help of a scraper and a dusting of flour, roll each portion into a smooth ball. Place a kitchen towel lightly over the ball(s). Let sit for 1 hour for freshly made dough or for 2–3 hours for chilled dough.
5. 45 minutes before baking, preheat the oven with your baking sheet or baking stone to 235°C fan (455°F/Gas 8).
6. Sprinkle a baking paddle or the back of a baking sheet generously with polenta (cornmeal) or semolina to prevent the dough from sticking. Press the dough into a flat circle, moving and rotating, making sure it isn't sticking to the paddle.
7. Spread a few teaspoons of olive oil on the dough and, working quickly, add your favourite toppings. Quickly, with the help of an offset spatula, transfer the pizza onto the heated surface. Bake in the preheated oven for 10–13 minutes, or until golden and the cheese is bubbling.

Tip For a classic tomato base, use the Simple Tomato Sauce recipe on page 215.

Chill
The dough can be kept in the fridge in an airtight container for up to 4 days.

Freeze
Freeze portions of dough in an airtight container for up to 6 months.

Defrost
Let the dough thaw overnight (or for at least 5 hours) in the fridge. Proceed from step 4.

SEEDY FILLED FLATBREADS

These filled flatbreads have become our go-to meal, especially on hectic evenings. The dough is a dream: you can pretty much forget about it in the fridge… and like a loyal friend, it's there for you when you need it. You can never have too many friends.

MAKES 10

VEGAN

500g (generous 3½ cups) plain (all-purpose) flour

75g (½ cup plus 1 tbsp) chickpea flour, sifted

7g sachet (¼oz envelope/ 2 tsp) active dried yeast

1 tsp caster (granulated) sugar

2¼ tsp salt

300ml (1¼ cups) water

2 tbsp olive oil, plus extra for greasing and frying

fillings of your choice, such as grated cheese or vegan cheese, roasted vegetables and herbs

2 tbsp poppy seeds

2 tbsp sesame seeds

2 tbsp sunflower seeds

2 tbsp linseeds (flaxseeds) or chia seeds

1. Combine the flours with the yeast, sugar and salt. Mix the water and oil, and add to the flour mixture. Using a stand mixer, knead for 4 minutes. The dough will be soft.

2. Grease a bowl lightly with oil and return the dough to it. Cover airtight and let rise either on your work surface for 2 hours or in the fridge for at least 6 hours.

3. When ready to use, prepare some fillings of your choice. Break off a piece of dough – I use 100g (3½oz) per flatbread. The dough will be soft and a bit sticky. Spread some seeds on your work surface (these also prevent sticking). Flatten out the dough on top of the seeds into a circle, about 12.5–14cm (5–5½in) in diameter.

4. Place some fillings in the middle of the dough. Bring the edges of the dough to the middle and join them. Using a rolling pin, flatten the filled dough again, to a disc, about 1cm (½in) thick.

5. Heat some olive oil in a heavy frying pan over medium heat and place a flatbread in the frying pan. Cook for about 4 minutes on each side. Repeat for each flatbread. Sprinkle some more seeds on top and enjoy!

Chill
The dough can be kept in the fridge in an airtight container for up to 5 days.

Freeze
Freeze portions of dough in an airtight container for up to 6 months.

Defrost
Let the dough thaw overnight (or for at least 5 hours) in the fridge. Proceed from step 3.

BERCHES WITH SWEET POTATO

Inspired by the classic German Jewish Sabbath bread, I use this dough as a blank canvas for the addition of herbs, raisins, walnuts or chopped onions, olives or basil.

**MAKES 2 LOAVES
OR 20 KNOTS**

400g (14oz/3 cups) peeled and chopped sweet potatoes

75ml (⅓ cup) olive oil, plus extra for kneading

1kg (7¼ cups) strong white bread flour

12g (3 tsp) active dried yeast

1½ tbsp salt

1 tsp caster (granulated) sugar

grated zest of 1 orange

350ml (1½ cups) water

For topping

1 egg, lightly beaten with 1 tsp water

sesame seeds or raw quinoa

1. Cook the sweet potatoes in a pan of salted boiling water until soft. Drain and mash with the oil, then set aside.
2. In a large bowl, combine the flour, yeast, salt, sugar and orange zest.
3. Using a stand mixer fitted with a dough hook, knead the sweet potatoes and the water into the flour mixture for 2–3 minutes until smooth. This is a soft dough.
4. Turn the dough out onto a lightly oiled work surface and knead it a bit by hand. If you want to bake it in a few hours, place the dough into a bowl, cover with a damp kitchen towel and let rise for 1–2 hours until doubled in bulk. Alternatively, set the dough in an airtight container to rest in the fridge overnight.
5. For a loaf, take half the dough. Divide it into three or more pieces and roll out each piece to a long strand. Press the ends together and begin plaiting (braiding). Tuck the ends of the bread under it at the beginning and end of the braid so the loaf won't open during baking. For little knots, use about 100g (3½oz) per knot. Roll into a strand and tie a knot!
6. Preheat the oven to 190°C fan (375°F/Gas 5) and line a baking sheet with parchment. Put the loaf or knots on the baking sheet, brush with the egg glaze and let rise for 30 minutes.
7. Brush again with the egg, sprinkle with sesame seeds or quinoa and bake until golden; 30 minutes for a loaf and 15 minutes for knots. Tap the underside of the loaf; if it sounds hollow, it's done. Let cool on a wire rack.

Chill
The dough can be kept in an airtight container in the fridge for 2 days. Remove the amount needed and bring to room temperature in a covered bowl.

Freeze
Divide the dough in half or into knot portions after the first rise, and freeze each portion, wrapped airtight, for up to 6 months.

Defrost
Let the dough thaw overnight (or for at least 5 hours) in the fridge. Proceed from step 4.

BEETROOT BREAD

This bread is fantastic! After my husband got over its shocking colour, we enjoyed it slathered with cream cheese and topped off with herring, red onions and dill. Delicious!

MAKES 2 LOAVES

VEGAN

450g (1lb/1⅔ cups) peeled and chopped beetroot (beets)

1 tsp freshly squeezed lemon juice

575g (4 cups plus 2 tbsp) strong white bread flour, plus extra for dusting

7g sachet (¼oz envelope/ 2 tsp) active dried yeast

2 tsp salt

125ml (½ cup) water

olive oil, for greasing

semolina or polenta (cornmeal), for sprinkling

1. Cook the chopped beetroot (beets) in a pan of boiling water until soft. Drain, then purée with the lemon juice and set aside to cool slightly.
2. In a large bowl, combine the flour, yeast and salt. Add the beetroot purée and water. Using a stand mixer fitted with a dough hook, knead for 4 minutes. The dough is very soft. Use a bench scraper to help shape it into a ball and place into a clean and lightly oiled bowl. Cover airtight.
3. Put the bowl in a warm place to rise for 1–2 hours until doubled in bulk. Or let half rise now to bake today and pop half in the fridge or freezer for another day.
4. 2 hours before baking your bread, line a shallow bowl, approximately the size of loaf you'd like, with a dry kitchen towel and sprinkle generously with flour.
5. Divide the dough in half, if not already done so (chill or freeze the other portion). On a *very* lightly floured surface, gently flatten the dough, pull the sides up to the middle and pinch together to form a ball. Place this ball, seam-side up, into the prepared bowl. Cover with a dry kitchen towel and let rise at room temperature for 1½ hours.
6. 45 minutes prior to baking, place a baking sheet in the oven. Place a small heatproof bowl filled with water on the floor of the oven and preheat the oven to 225°C fan (430°F/Gas 7) for at least 45 minutes. The intense heat of the baking sheet and the humidity from the water aid in creating a perfect, crusty bread.
7. Remove the baking sheet from the oven and sprinkle with semolina or polenta (cornmeal). Turn the dough directly onto it and, with a sharp knife, slash the top.
8. Return the baking sheet to the oven and bake for 25 minutes until the bread has risen and sounds hollow when the underside is tapped. Let cool on a wire rack.

Chill
The dough can be kept in the fridge in an airtight container for 4 days. The colour can fade with time.

Freeze
Once the dough has risen in a warm place for 1–2 hours, wrap airtight and freeze for up to 6 months.

Defrost
Let the dough thaw overnight (or for at least 5 hours) in the fridge. Proceed from step 5.

POPPY SEED ROLLS

I make these poppy seed and onion-filled rolls in a loaf pan, then ever-so-gently pull them apart to serve. Delicious!

MAKES 10

350ml (1½ cups) whole milk

75g (5 tbsp) butter, cold

525g (3¾ cups) plain (all-purpose) flour

7g sachet (¼oz envelope/ 2 tsp) active dried yeast

20g (1 tbsp plus 2 tsp) Demerara (raw) sugar

1½ tsp salt

butter, for greasing

Filling

½ onion, finely chopped

2 tbsp poppy seeds, plus 2 tbsp for sprinkling

For brushing

40g (3 tbsp) butter, melted

¼ tsp sea salt

1. Scald the milk (see page 159). Add the cold butter to the scalded milk and let it melt. Let cool to room temperature; this may take up to 15 minutes.
2. In a large mixing bowl, combine the flour, yeast, sugar and salt. Add the cooled milk to flour mixture (do not add the milk to the yeast until it is room temperature, or you will kill the yeast). With a stand mixer fitted with a dough hook, knead the dough for 3–4 minutes. Turn the dough out onto a lightly floured surface and knead for a few more minutes. Lightly butter a large bowl. Shape the dough into a ball, place into the buttered bowl and cover airtight.
3. To bake the same day, put the bowl in a warm place to rise until doubled in bulk, about 45 minutes.
4. Butter an 11 x 29cm (4¼ x 11½in) loaf pan or 20cm (8in) round baking pan.
5. Make the filling by simply combining the onion and poppy seeds in a small bowl. Combine the melted butter with the salt for brushing.
6. After the first rise, divide the dough into ten equal portions.
7. Flatten a piece of dough to 7.5 x 10cm (3 x 4in). Place a teaspoon of filling in the middle, then encase in the dough. Roll into a round shape and place in the baking pan. Brush with melted butter and sprinkle poppy seeds on top.
8. Preheat the oven to 200°C fan (400°F/Gas 6). Let the rolls rise for 25 minutes.
9. Bake in the preheated oven for 33–36 minutes, or until golden. Remove from the oven and brush again with melted butter. Let cool a little in the pan, then enjoy!

Chill

The dough can be kept in the fridge in an airtight container for up to 2 days.

Freeze

The dough can be frozen, wrapped airtight, for 6 months. Alternatively, freeze the formed rolls before the second rise.

Defrost

Let the dough thaw overnight (or for at least 5 hours) in the fridge. Proceed from step 4.

GARLIC AND HERB WOVEN BREAD

Two things to know about this recipe: 1) Homemade bread remains fresh longer than store-bought. 2) Garlic and herbs are seductively addictive.

MAKES 2 LOAVES

50g (3 tbsp plus 1 tsp) butter, plus extra for greasing

500ml (2 cups) buttermilk

500g (generous 3½ cups) plain (all-purpose) flour, plus extra for dusting

150g (1 cup plus 2 tbsp) whole-grain flour

7g sachet (¼oz envelope/ 2 tsp) active dried yeast

¼ tsp bicarbonate of soda (baking soda)

2¼ tsp salt

2 tsp caster (granulated) sugar

1 x quantity Cheesy Garlic Herb Butter (see page 214)

1. Melt the butter in a pan over a low heat. Add the buttermilk and gently heat until warm but not too hot.
2. In a large mixing bowl, combine the flours, yeast, bicarbonate of soda (baking soda), salt and sugar. Add the buttermilk mixture.
3. Transfer to a stand mixer fitted with a dough hook and knead for about 4 minutes.
4. Turn the dough out onto a lightly floured board and knead for a few minutes more. The dough is quite soft; don't be tempted to knead in too much extra flour.
5. Lightly butter a large bowl. Shape the dough into a ball, place into the buttered bowl and cover airtight. To bake the same day, put the bowl in a warm place to rise until doubled in bulk, about 45 minutes. Or divide the dough in half and let one half rise to bake today and pop half in the fridge or freezer.
6. Lightly butter a 13 x 23cm (5 x 9in) loaf pan and line with parchment.
7. Divide the dough in half, if not already done (chill or freeze the other portion). On a lightly floured surface, roll out the dough to a 30cm (12in) square. Spread the herb butter over the dough and roll up like a sausage. The filling is strong – a little goes a long way!
8. Cut down the middle of the sausage. Twist the halves around each other, tuck the edge of the dough under and set into the loaf pan. Let rise for 30 minutes.
9. Preheat the oven to 190°C fan (375°F/Gas 5).
10. Bake the loaf in the preheated oven until the bread is golden and springs back when lightly touched, about 35 minutes. Let the loaf cool in the pan for a few minutes before turning out onto a wire rack to cool completely.

Chill
The dough can be kept in the fridge in an airtight container for up to 3 days.

Freeze
The dough can be kept in the freezer, wrapped airtight, for up to 6 months.

Defrost
Let the dough thaw overnight (or for at least 5 hours) in the fridge. Proceed from step 6.

PARSNIP MISO CINNAMON SWIRL BREAD

Parsnips? Miso? Cinnamon? Let me explain. The yeast loves the parsnips because they're sweet and starchy. The parsnips love the miso caramel because it's salty and sweet. And everything loves the earthiness of the cinnamon. Bicarbonate of soda (baking soda) works with the buttermilk to give the bread a light and spongy texture. Pictured page 154–155.

MAKES 2 LOAVES

375g (13oz) parsnips, washed and cut into chunks

1 tbsp caster (granulated) sugar

1 tbsp vegetable oil

50g (3 tbsp plus 1 tsp) butter, plus extra for greasing

1 egg

350ml (1½ cups) buttermilk

450g (3⅓ cups) plain (all-purpose) flour

150g (scant 1½ cups) porridge oats

2 tsp muscovado sugar

7g sachet (¼oz envelope/ 2 tsp) active dried yeast

¾ tsp salt

¼ tsp bicarbonate of soda (baking soda)

2–4 tbsp Miso Caramel with Sea Salt (see page 203)

Filling, for 1 loaf

60g (½ stick) butter, softened

60g (generous ⅓ cup) light muscovado sugar or brown sugar

2 tsp ground cinnamon

big pinch of salt

2 tbsp plain (all-purpose) flour

handful of raisins (optional)

1. Preheat the oven to 210°C fan (410°F/Gas 6) and line a baking sheet with parchment. Toss the parsnips with the caster (granulated) sugar and vegetable oil and arrange them on the lined baking sheet.

2. Roast in the preheated oven for 15–20 minutes until golden.

3. Transfer the cooked parsnips to a bowl, add the butter and purée until smooth. Mix in the egg and buttermilk. Set aside.

4. In a large bowl, combine the flour, oats, muscovado sugar, yeast, salt and bicarbonate of soda (baking soda). Using a stand mixer fitted with a dough hook, knead the parsnip mixture with the flour mixture for 4 minutes until the dough is elastic and supple. Turn out onto lightly floured work surface and continue to knead by hand for several minutes. Smear the inside of a large bowl with butter, add the dough and cover airtight.

5. Put the bowl in a warm place to rise until doubled in bulk, about 45 minutes. Or divide the dough in half and let one half rise to bake today and pop half in the fridge or freezer.

6. Stir together the ingredients for the filling and set aside. Lightly butter and line a 13 x 23cm (5 x 9in) loaf pan with parchment.

7. When the dough has sufficiently risen, knock it back (punch it down) gently and turn out onto a lightly floured work surface. Divide it in half, if you've not already done so (chill or freeze the other portion).

8. Roll out half the dough into a 25 x 30cm (10 x 12in) rectangle. Evenly spread 1–2 tablespoons of miso caramel on the dough, followed by the cinnamon and sugar filling. Roll up tightly like a log.

9. Using a very sharp knife, *bravely* cut down the middle of the bread, leaving 2cm (¾in) attached at the top. It is important to work quickly here otherwise the filling will run out and, sometimes, working swiftly makes everything easier. Twist the two halves over each other, tuck the ends under and place the dough into the prepared loaf pan. If there are any raisins on the surface, tuck them into the dough (they can easily burn during baking).

10. Let rise a second time for 25 minutes. Preheat the oven to 185°C fan (365°F/ Gas 4). Bake in the preheated oven for 37–40 minutes. Check the colour of the bread after 25 minutes and cover with parchment if getting too dark. Test by lightly pressing on the bread; when it springs back, it's done.

11. Remove from the oven and let cool for 5 minutes in the loaf pan before removing to completely cool on a rack.

Chill
The dough can be kept in the fridge in an airtight container for up to 2 days.

Freeze
After the first rise, the dough can be kept in the freezer, wrapped airtight, for up to 6 months.

Defrost
Let the dough thaw overnight (or for at least 5 hours) in the fridge. Proceed from step 6.

HONEY LEMON CHALLAH

This is my final opus: a flavourful composition of fennel, honey and lemon. Add the billowy texture of the bread and you've got a sensory symphony.

**MAKES 2 LOAVES
OR 20 KNOTS**

1kg (7¼ cups) strong white bread flour

12g (3 tsp) active dried yeast

10g (2¼ tsp) salt

1 tsp fennel seeds, ground

50g (scant ¼ cup) caster (superfine) sugar

4 eggs

100ml (scant ½ cup) vegetable or olive oil, plus extra for coating

50g (3 tbsp) runny honey

350ml (1½ cups) water

grated zest of 1 lemon

For topping

1 egg, beaten

sesame seeds and/or poppy seeds

1. In a large bowl, combine the flour, yeast, salt, ground fennel seeds and sugar.
2. Whisk the eggs together with the vegetable oil, honey, water and lemon zest.
3. Using a stand mixer fitted with a dough hook, knead the liquids into the flour, adding 1–2 tablespoons more water if needed. Knead for 4 minutes until smooth.
4. Knead the dough a bit by hand to get a feeling for its texture! If you want to bake it today, place the dough into a bowl lightly coated with a few drops of olive oil, and cover with a damp kitchen towel. Let rise for 1–2 hours until doubled in bulk. Or divide the dough in half and let one half rise to bake today and pop half in the fridge or freezer.
5. For a loaf, take half the dough (chill or freeze the rest) and divide it into three pieces (or more, depending upon your plaiting/braiding skills). Roll out each piece to a long strand. Press the ends together and begin plaiting. Tuck the ends of the bread under it at the beginning and end of the braid so the loaf won't open during baking. For little knots, use about 100g (3½oz/½ cup) per knot. Roll into a strand and tie a knot.
6. Preheat the oven to 190°C fan (375°F/Gas 5) and line a baking sheet with parchment. Put the loaf or knots on the baking sheet. For a beautiful, golden crust, brush lightly with the beaten egg and let rise for 30 minutes.
7. Brush again with the egg wash, sprinkle with sesame seeds and poppy seeds, and bake the loaf for about 30 minutes until golden, or the knots for about 15 minutes. Check by tapping the underside of the loaf; if it sounds hollow, it's done. Let cool completely on a rack before enjoying.

Chill

The dough can be kept in the fridge in an airtight container for up to 3 days.

Freeze

Freeze after the first rise, braided or not, for up to 6 months.

Defrost

Let the dough thaw overnight (or for at least 5 hours) in the fridge. Proceed from step 5.

DANISH PASTRY DOUGH

A Danish pastry dough needs to be in everyone's repertoire. Why? Because it is delicious, versatile and a little effort goes a long way. So make the effort, reap the benefits, win friends and maybe even inspire people along the way!

MAKES 24

300ml (1¼ cups) whole milk

525g (3¾ cups) strong white bread flour or plain (all-purpose) flour, plus extra for dusting

10g (2½ tsp) active dried yeast

50g (¼ cup) caster (granulated) sugar

1 tsp salt

½ tsp ground cardamom

1 egg

1 egg yolk (use the white in the Marzipan Filling on page 160 or freeze it)

finely grated zest of 1 lemon

250g (2 sticks) butter, very cold

1. Scald the milk, then let it cool to room temperature (see opposite).
2. In a large mixing bowl, combine the flour, yeast, sugar, salt and cardamom. Set aside.
3. Whisk together the milk, egg, egg yolk and lemon zest. Add the liquids to the flour mixture. With a stand mixer fitted with a dough hook, knead the dough for about 3 minutes. Be patient. This dough is a bit soft. This is correct. Don't be tempted to add more flour.
4. Turn the dough out onto a lightly floured work surface and, with the help of a bench scraper, continue to knead for several minutes by hand. The dough will remain rather soft. Wrap the dough in parchment and place in the fridge for 15 minutes to cool before proceeding.
5. Place the butter between two sheets of lightly floured parchment. Using a rolling pin, pound on, then roll out the butter to a flat 20cm (8in) square. Wrap in parchment and set in the fridge or freezer for 10 minutes.
6. Remove the dough from the fridge, place it on a floured work surface and roll out to a 40cm (16in) square. Place the butter in the centre of the dough. Fold the ends of dough in towards the centre to make a package. Gently press the ends into the dough to seal.
7. Keep the work surface dusted with flour. Roll the dough out to a rectangle, about 45cm (18in) long. Fold one end of the dough into the centre, then the other over it, like a letter, to form a square. You will have three layers of dough. Wrap in parchment and place in the fridge to rest for 25 minutes.
8. Roll out the dough a second time into a rectangle. Repeat the folding process twice more, letting the dough rest between each time. Keep track of how many times you have rolled out and turned the dough; you want to do it a total of four times.

9. At this stage, the dough can be wrapped airtight and kept in the fridge for up to 2 days. I usually divide the dough in half, bake half now and store the other half in the fridge to bake fresh the next day. You can also freeze the dough (in two portions) at this stage, but it is most convenient to freeze it once shaped.

Scalding milk To scald milk, bring it just to the boil, then allow it to cool. Scalding denatures the serum protein in milk, which has a weakening effect on gluten. We need the gluten strength for the dough structure. Scalding milk also deactivates the protease enzyme that can slow down the yeast. So don't skip scalding the milk.

Chill
The dough can be kept in the fridge, wrapped airtight, for up to 2 days.

Freeze
The dough can be divided in half, rolled out to a 25 x 40cm (10 x 16in) rectangle on a lightly floured piece of parchment, topped with another piece of parchment, and rolled up like a log. Wrap each log airtight before freezing.

Defrost
Let a log of dough thaw overnight (or for at least 5 hours) in the fridge, then proceed with the recipe. Let individual portions thaw for several hours in the fridge, then proceed with the second rise on a baking sheet.

MARZIPAN-FILLED DANISH PASTRIES

Newsflash: You can make marzipan out of any kind of nut or a mixture of nuts. Time to go to town with this! These marzipan-filled Danish pastries are the perfect weekend breakfast or elevenses treat. Pictured page 164–165.

MAKES 12

½ x quantity Danish Pastry Dough (see page 158)

100g (⅔ cup) raisins, soaked in warm water for 30 minutes, well drained

1 egg, lightly beaten, to glaze

Filling

250g (2 cups) mixed nuts, such as pistachios, almonds and/or walnuts

125g (generous 1 cup) icing (confectioners') sugar

1 egg white

1 tsp vanilla extract (see page 202, optional)

pinch of salt

25g (scant ¼ stick) butter, softened

1. To make the filling, using a food processor, finely grind the nuts. Add the icing (confectioners') sugar followed by the egg white, vanilla extract, salt and butter. Continue to grind for several minutes. Transfer to a bowl.

2. On a lightly floured work surface, roll out the dough to a 25 x 40cm (10 x 16in) rectangle. Smear the nut filling evenly over the dough. Sprinkle the nut filling with hydrated raisins.

3. Roll the dough up evenly and tightly, like a rug. Cut into 1.5cm (⅝in) slices. There will be a 'tail' on each slice – simply tuck the end of the outer coil under the pastry so it doesn't open during baking. Place on a baking sheet about 4cm (1½in) apart. Let rise for 30 minutes.

4. Preheat the oven to 195°C fan (380°F/Gas 5).

5. Brush the pastries with beaten egg and bake in the preheated oven for about 15 minutes, checking after 10 minutes for colour – if the pastry is getting too dark, cover with parchment and continue to bake until cooked.

6. Let cool on baking sheet for 10 minutes before transferring to a wire rack to cool completely.

Chill

Once formed, the pastries can be kept in the fridge, wrapped airtight, for 24 hours.

Freeze

The pastries can be frozen once formed (before rising) for up to 4 months.

Defrost

Let thaw for several hours in the fridge, then proceed with the second rise on a baking sheet.

CHOCOLATE AND HAZELNUT-FILLED DANISH PASTRIES

I am in love with this indulgent chocolatey filling. It's like a high-end hazelnut spread... but even better! It partners so well with homemade Danish dough to create the most irresistible pastry. Breakfast will never be the same again! Pictured page 164–165.

MAKES 12

½ x quantity Danish Pastry Dough (see page 158)

1 egg, lightly beaten, to glaze

100g (¾ cup) hazelnuts, chopped and lightly roasted

Filling

175g (1½ sticks) butter, softened

75g (½ cup) dark brown muscovado sugar

75g (scant ⅔ cup) icing (confectioners') sugar

45g (½ cup) unsweetened cocoa powder

1 tsp vanilla extract (see page 202)

pinch of salt

1. To make the filling, using a stand mixer or hand-held electric whisk, combine the butter, sugars, cocoa, vanilla extract and salt until well mixed.
2. On a lightly floured work surface, roll out the dough to a 25 x 40cm (10 x 16in) rectangle. Smear the chocolate filling evenly over the dough. Sprinkle the chocolate filling with toasted hazelnuts.
3. Roll the dough up evenly and tightly, like a rug. Cut into 1.5cm (⅝in) slices. There will be a 'tail' on each slice – simply tuck the end of the outer coil under the pastry so it doesn't open during baking. Place on a baking sheet about 4cm (1½in) apart. Let rise for 30 minutes.
4. Preheat the oven to 195°C fan (380°F/Gas 5).
5. Brush the pastries with beaten egg and bake for about 15 minutes, checking after 10 minutes for colour – if the pastry is getting too dark, cover with parchment and continue to bake until cooked.
6. Let cool on baking sheet for 10 minutes before transferring to a wire rack to cool completely.

Chill

Once formed, the pastries can be kept in the fridge, wrapped airtight, for 24 hours.

Freeze

The pastries can be frozen once formed (before rising) for up to 4 months.

Defrost

Let thaw for several hours in the fridge, then proceed with the second rise on a baking sheet.

CRESCENT ROLLS

A croissant dough is a laminated dough like the Danish but doesn't contain eggs. For this reason, we're baking breakfast crescents! I love them with an almond marzipan filling (the German in me). You can also simply leave them *au naturel*. Roll them, cut them, shape them and pop them in the freezer and you'll have fresh crescents for breakfast without ever having to put your shoes on. Pictured page 164–165.

MAKES 12

½ x quantity Danish Pastry Dough (see page 158)

plain (all-purpose) flour, for dusting

1 egg, beaten, for brushing

flaked (sliced) almonds, to decorate

Filling

150g (5oz) marzipan

3 tbsp ground almonds

3 tbsp milk

a few scrapings of lemon or orange zest

1. Combine the marzipan, ground almonds, milk and zest for the filling and mix well. Set aside. Line two baking sheets with parchment.
2. Divide the portion of dough in half and return the other half to the fridge to use later.
3. On a lightly floured work surface, roll out the dough to a rectangle, 12 x 36cm (5 x 14in). Cut the dough into thirds to create three 12cm (5in) squares).
4. Cut each square in half on the diagonal to give you six triangles.
5. Gently pull and stretch the dough to make it a bit longer and wider.
6. Divide the filling into 12 small sausage shapes. Place a small sausage-shape of filling at the wide end of a triangle of dough and roll it up. Place on the baking sheet. Make sure the crescent is sitting on top of the tip of the triangle; this keeps the shape intact during baking. Now bend the tips of the crescent towards the middle, to form a nice crescent shape. Repeat with the remaining triangles.
7. Take the rest of the dough from the fridge and repeat to make another six crescents, placing the crescents 4cm (1½in) apart on the baking sheets. Let them rise at room temperature for about 30 minutes.
8. Preheat the oven to 210°C fan (410°F/Gas 6). Brush each crescent with beaten egg and sprinkle with flaked (sliced) almonds.
9. Bake in the preheated oven for about 12 minutes, or until golden. Let cool on the baking sheet for 10 minutes, then transfer to a wire rack to cool completely.

Chill
Once formed, the pastries can be kept in the fridge, wrapped airtight, for 24 hours.

Freeze
Freeze the pastries before the last rise on a plate. When frozen, transfer to an airtight bag and freeze for up to 6 months.

Defrost
Let the dough thaw overnight (or for at least 5 hours) in the fridge. Proceed from step 8.

CHOCOLATE DANISH

Pain au chocolat is made with croissant dough, which, although laminated like this Danish dough, contains no eggs. But we're going to afford ourselves the freedom to do as we please and disregard tradition. Voilà, *Danois au chocolat*, Danish pastry filled with chocolate, just the way you like it! Pictured page 164–165.

MAKES 12

2 x 100g (3½oz) bars plain (semi-sweet) chocolate

½ x quantity Danish Pastry Dough (see page 158)

plain (all-purpose) flour, for dusting

1 egg, for brushing

1. Cut each bar of chocolate into six (rectangular) pieces and set aside. Line two baking sheets with parchment.
2. Divide the portion of dough in half and return half of it to the fridge to use later.
3. On a lightly floured work surface, roll out the dough to a rectangle, 10cm (4in) wide and 42cm (16½in) long. Cut the dough in half. You will have two sheets of dough now, 10cm (4in) wide and 21cm (8¼in) long. Cut each sheet into three pieces. You will have six rectangles, 10 x 7cm (4 x 2¾in).
4. Gently pull and stretch the dough to make it a bit longer and wider.
5. Place a row of chocolate on the wide end of the dough and loosely roll it up. Place on the baking sheet, seam-side down.
6. Repeat with the rest of the dough, placing the pastries 4cm (1½in) apart on the baking sheets. Let them rise at room temperature for about 30 minutes.
7. Preheat the oven to 200°C fan (400°F/Gas 6). Brush each pastry with the beaten egg.
8. Bake in the preheated oven for about 14 minutes, or until golden. Let cool on the baking sheet for 10 minutes before transferring to a wire rack to cool completely.

Chill
Once formed, the pastries can be kept in the fridge, wrapped airtight, for 24 hours.

Freeze
Freeze the pastries before the last rise on a plate. When frozen, transfer to an airtight bag and freeze for up to 6 months.

Defrost
Let the dough thaw overnight (or for at least 5 hours) in the fridge. Proceed from step 7.

PAS

TRY

PASTRY is simply one of those things that is much better homemade. Many people think nothing of using frozen shortcrust pastry from the supermarket, which is quick and easy, but tasteless. Today is your lucky day! Set yourself free. You've just won the recipe lottery and will never have to use generic, store-bought crusts again.

HANDLE THE DOUGH LIGHTLY, AS IF IT WERE SO HOT, IT WOULD BURN YOUR FINGERS!

PASTRY SECRETS

You might think anything that is so delicious, so special, must be difficult to make. Wrong. Follow a few simple rules, and you're home free. And hey – you can make it all by hand, no fancy kitchen equipment needed.

Whether you're making a classic pie dough, a cream cheese dough or a polenta (cornmeal) crostata, all these doughs have a few things in common. Use very cold fat, very cold water and do not overwork the dough. Unlike a yeast dough that likes warmth and to be kneaded, a pastry dough only likes to be handled until it comes together. Keep it light, keep it cold. Make sure you can see butter marbled throughout the shortcrust. Handle the dough lightly, as if it were so hot, it would burn your fingers!

Rough puff, mock puff, whatever you want to call it, a quick and easy method of making your own laminated pastry is a culinary epiphany. With a little more effort than with a classic pie dough, the light and flaky layers of these laminated doughs are gonna' make you **the star** in your kitchen.

Here are some tricks of the trade
- if you like a subtle nutty flavour, you can swap out some of the plain (all-purpose) flour for whole-wheat flour, but no more than 25 per cent (whole-wheat flour is weightier than plain flour, has less gluten and absorbs more water, which can make it a bit trickier to work with)
- use only a light dusting of flour when rolling out the dough – do not try and compensate for a warm, sticky dough with the use of extra flour, which will result in a poor texture
- if you need some extra time or your kitchen is warm and your dough gets soft and sticky, remember the fridge is your friend – pop the dough in the fridge, give it a 15-minute rest, then proceed
- the simpler the dough, the quicker it oxidizes, so use a shortcrust within 48 hours or freeze it (for quick thawing, I like to freeze mine already rolled out)
- it is preferable to freeze the dough as opposed to freezing the baked pastry (a baked pastry can get soggy when thawing, whereas the raw dough remains perfect)
- use a bit of soda water in the rough puff – the steam created from the carbonation when baking results in particularly delicate and flaky layers
- practice makes perfect

FLAKY SHORTCRUST PASTRY

This is my favourite (and soon to be your favourite!) shortcrust recipe, which is perfect for pie or quiche. Easy to make, delicious to eat, it will never fail you. Two important points: use cold butter and lard or vegetable shortening, really cold water, and do NOT overwork the dough. Less is more. Never knead a shortcrust as you would a yeast dough.

**MAKES 850G
(1LB 14OZ)**

200g (1¾ sticks) butter, very cold

80g (⅓ cup) lard or 80g (generous ⅓ cup) vegetable shortening, very cold

150ml (½ cup plus 2 tbsp) water, very cold

420g (3 cups) plain (all-purpose) flour, plus extra for dusting

½–2 tsp white (granulated) sugar (use a bit more sugar if the dough is for a sweet pie)

1 tsp salt

1. Cut the butter and lard or vegetable shortening into thin slices and put in the fridge, along with the water while you weigh out all the other ingredients. It is really important that they are cold.
2. In a large bowl combine flour, sugar and salt. Add the butter and shortening or lard to the flour. Use a stand mixer or your fingertips to break up the fat into coarse pieces about the size of large peas. You still want to see bits of fat and butter! Add the cold water and, using a fork, barely mix to combine.
3. Turn the dough onto a lightly floured work surface, and just lightly knead together. Divide in half, and quickly shape each half into a roughly shaped circle. The secret to a flaky crust is not just cold butter and water, but also not handling the dough too much.
4. Wrap each disc in parchment and refrigerate for about 1 hour.

Chill
The dough can be kept in the fridge, wrapped airtight, for up to 2 days.

Freeze
The dough can be kept in the freezer, wrapped airtight, for 6 months.

Defrost
Let thaw overnight in the fridge before use.

ONION QUICHE

If you've never made quiche before, now's the time to start. It's simply a savoury pie with a filling suspended in an egg custard. A little effort goes a long way! Pictured page 171.

SERVES 8

½ x quantity Flaky Shortcrust Pastry (see page 170)

plain (all-purpose) flour, for dusting

2 tbsp olive oil

30g (2 tbsp) butter

800g (1lb 12oz) small onions, halved

pinch of sugar

2–3 tbsp finely chopped fresh herbs, such as parsley, marjoram, thyme

100g (1 cup) coarsely grated Cheddar, Gruyère or your favourite hard cheese

2–3 eggs

250–375ml (1–1½ cups) whole milk, cream or a mixture of both

freshly grated nutmeg, to taste

salt and pepper

1. Preheat the oven to 200°C fan (400°F/Gas 6). We need to blind bake the crust.
2. Roll out the pastry on a lightly floured work surface until it is 3–4mm (⅛in) thick. Continue to work sparingly with flour on your rolling pin and on your work surface, making sure that the dough does not stick to either. Work quickly and keep the work surface and rolling pin free of softened dough. Dough sticks to dough! If things are sticking – put the dough in the fridge for 15 minutes.
3. Place the rolled-out dough into a 23–25cm (9–10in) tart pan and gently press the dough into the bottom and sides of the pan. No need to butter the pan. Prick the dough lightly with a fork and chill for at least 15 minutes. Line with parchment and pie weights or dried beans. Blind bake for 10 minutes, then carefully remove the parchment and pie weights. Let cool slightly on a wire rack.
4. Heat the oil and butter in a frying pan and sauté the onion halves on one side for 5 minutes. Add the sugar and a pinch of salt, and continue to cook for 5 minutes more. Turn the onions over and cook on the other side for 10 minutes. Remove from the heat and set aside.
5. Lower the oven temperature to 190°C fan (375°F/Gas 5). Sprinkle half the grated cheese and half the herbs on the pre-baked crust. Place the cooked onions on top. Season with a bit of salt and pepper. Mix the eggs with the cream or milk. Add some nutmeg, salt and pepper to taste. Pour the custard over the vegetables and sprinkle the remaining grated cheese and herbs on top.
6. Bake in the lower third of the oven for 45 minutes. Check after 25 minutes and cover with parchment if necessary, but bake for the final 5 minutes uncovered.

Tip As a rule of thumb for quiche, use the ratio 1 egg to 125ml (½ cup) cream or milk.

FRUIT PIE

Nothing but nothing can compete with a homemade pie. You can make it with a closed crust with steam vents, a lattice crust or a streusel topping (see page 211). Pictured page 171.

SERVES 8

6 apples (about 1.36kg/3lb), peeled, cored and sliced

1 tsp freshly squeezed lemon juice

30–40g (4–5 tbsp) plain (all-purpose) flour, plus extra for dusting

80–100g (6 tbsp–½ cup) caster (granulated) sugar, to taste

pinch of ground cinnamon (optional)

grated zest of 1 lemon (optional)

1 x quantity Flaky Shortcrust Pastry (see page 170)

1. Preheat the oven to 215°C fan (420°F/Gas 7). Have a 23–25cm (9–10in) pie pan ready for use. No need to butter it. Mix the sliced apples with the lemon juice, flour, sugar, cinnamon and lemon zest, if using. Set aside.
2. Divide the dough and keep one half in the fridge. Roll out the other half on a lightly floured work surface into a disc about 3–4mm (⅛in) thick. Work with a light dusting of flour on your rolling pin and on your work surface, making sure that the dough does not stick to either. Work quickly and keep the work surface and rolling pin free of softened dough. Dough sticks to dough! If things are sticking – put the dough in the fridge for 15 minutes.
3. Place the rolled-out dough into the pie pan and gently press it onto the bottom and sides of the pan. Fill the pie with the prepared fruit. Make sure that the shell is well filled with the fruit mixture; fruit shrinks during baking.
4. Roll out the other piece of dough into a disc about 3–4 mm (⅛in) thick.
5. Place the dough over the filling and trim the edges to size (I like using scissors for this), leaving a 1cm (½in) border to crimp. You can also use a knife. Crimp the edges together and make steam slits in the surface in a nice pattern.
6. Alternatively, cut the rolled-out dough into strips and weave a lattice crust – so much fun to do and easier than you think – or cut out shapes and make a crust by overlapping them. I like to use circles, hearts or squares.
7. Bake in the lower third of the preheated oven for 10 minutes, then reduce the heat to 190°C fan (375°F/Gas 5) and continue to bake for another 40 minutes. Check the colour after 30 minutes and cover with parchment if the pie is taking on colour too quickly. Bake for the final 5 minutes uncovered.

Variations You could use apples (or pears) and blackberries, blueberries or raspberries. Add the lemon juice to the fruit, followed by the flour, then the sugar. Cinnamon is always optional. If you are using berries, use up to 40g (5 tbsp) flour and 175g (¾ cup plus 2 tbsp) sugar, depending on their sweetness. Berries tend to give off a lot of liquid, which is why I combine them with apples or pears.

ROUGH PUFF PASTRY

OK. No more frozen puff pastry – ever. This mock puff or rough puff pastry tastes like classic puff, it looks like classic puff, but it is not going to rule your life for a day. The name of the game is coldness. If the dough gets sticky, immediately return it to the fridge for at least 20 minutes. If the butter melts, there will be no puffy layers.

**MAKES 600G
(1LB 5OZ)**

180g (1½ sticks) butter, cold

225g (1⅔ cups) plain (all-purpose) flour, plus extra for dusting

30g (3 tbsp plus 1 tsp) cornflour (cornstarch)

½ tsp salt

80ml (⅓ cup) water, cold

2 tbsp soda water, cold

70g (⅔ stick) butter, softened

1. Cut the cold butter into thin slices and put in the fridge.
2. Whisk together the flour, cornflour (cornstarch) and salt in a large bowl. Blend in the cold butter with your fingertips or a pastry blender until the mixture resembles very coarse meal. You want to see pieces of butter. Add the cold water and soda water, and stir with a fork just until a dough forms.
3. Turn the dough out onto a lightly floured work surface. Quickly knead the dough together and shape into a 10 x 15cm (4 x 6in) rectangle. Wrap the dough in parchment and refrigerate for 2 hours (or up to 24 hours). This resting time allows the dough to hydrate, the gluten to relax and the butter to re-stabilize.
4. On a lightly floured surface, roll out the dough into a 15 x 40cm (6 x 15in) rectangle, about 5mm (¼in) thick.
5. Spread half the softened butter on the upper two-thirds of the dough. Fold the bottom end of the dough into the centre, then the other end (with the butter) over it, like a letter, to make three layers of dough. Turn the dough so the closed edge is on the right. Roll out the dough to a rectangle again and smear the rest of the softened butter on the upper two-thirds of the dough. Fold the bottom third to the centre and the top third over it like a letter. Wrap and chill for 45 minutes.
6. Give it two or three more turns without the butter, letting it chill for 20 minutes before rolling and turning. *Et voilà!* Rough puff pastry!

Chill
You can store the dough in the fridge, wrapped airtight, for up to 2 days.

Freeze
Divide the dough in half. Roll each out to 25 x 40cm (10 x 16in), place on a lightly floured piece of parchment and roll up. Wrap airtight and freeze for 6 months.

Defrost
Let thaw for several hours in the fridge before using.

QUICK WHOLE-WHEAT ROUGH PUFF PASTRY

Make a rough puff pastry with (some) whole-wheat flour! The plain (all-purpose) flour keeps it light and flaky, whilst the whole-wheat flour gives it an appealing, nutty flavour.

**MAKES 700G
(1LB 8OZ)**

300g (2¾ sticks) butter, cold

225g (1⅔ cups) plain (all-purpose) flour, plus extra for dusting

75g (generous ½ cup) whole-wheat flour

¾ tsp salt

125ml (½ cup) water, cold

1. Cut the cold butter into thin slices and put in the fridge.
2. In a large bowl, whisk together the flours and salt. Blend in the cold butter with your fingertips, a pastry blender or a stand mixer until the mixture resembles very coarse meal. You want to see big pieces of butter. Add the cold water and stir with a fork just until the dough comes together. The dough will be very rough and shaggy.
3. Turn the dough onto a lightly floured surface and quickly knead together. Roll out into a rectangle, 20 x 35cm (8 x 14in); the dough will not be completely smooth.
4. Fold the top third of the dough to the middle. Fold the lower third over it, like you're folding a letter. Rotate the dough clockwise a quarter turn. This is the first turn.
5. Now repeat this process for the second turn; roll out the dough to a 20 x 35cm (8 x 14in) rectangle and fold it like a letter. You should have a perfect dough package now. Wrap in parchment and let it rest in the fridge for 30 minutes.
6. Roll out the dough to a 20 x 35cm (8 x 14in) rectangle. Fold it again like a letter. Rotate the dough clockwise a quarter turn (this is the third turn). Repeat this process of rolling and turning for the fourth turn. You should have a smooth dough package now. Wrap the dough in parchment and chill for 1 hour.
7. Repeat this process of rolling and turning for the fifth and sixth turns. You will have a perfect dough package now. Wrap the dough in parchment and chill for at least 1 hour. It needs to be well chilled before it can be rolled out.

Chill
You can store the dough in the fridge, wrapped airtight, for up to 2 days.

Freeze
Divide the dough in half. Roll each out to 25 x 40cm (10 x 16in), place on a lightly floured piece of parchment and roll up. Wrap airtight and freeze for 6 months.

Defrost
Let thaw for several hours in the fridge before using.

FRUIT TART WITH CHEESE FILLING

I have never been a fan of fruit with whipped cream but strangely, I would never say
no to a fruit tart with a mascarpone filling. We humans are so complex sometimes.

SERVES 8

½ x quantity Rough Puff
Pastry (see page 174)

plain (all-purpose) flour, for
dusting

cold water

5 tbsp apricot jam (jelly)

crème fraîche, to serve
(optional)

Filling

175g (¾ cup) cream cheese
or mascarpone

3 tbsp icing (confectioners')
sugar

1 tbsp plain (all-purpose)
flour or cornflour
(cornstarch)

a few scrapings of fresh
lemon or orange zest
(optional)

3 apples, pears or fresh figs
(approx. 600g (1lb 5oz)
of fruit)

1 egg, mixed with 1 tsp water

1 tbsp Demerara (raw) sugar

1. Brush a bit of water onto a baking sheet, then line with parchment. This creates
   steam while baking.
2. Keep the surface and rolling pin lightly dusted with flour. Roll out the dough to
   a rectangle, 22 x 32cm (8½ x 12½in) and place on the parchment. If at any
   point you feel the dough sticking, put it back in the fridge to cool for 15 minutes.
   Using a ruler, even up the sides so they are straight.
3. Have a small glass of cold water and a pastry brush ready. Cut strips of dough
   1cm (½in) wide from all four sides. Lightly brush the sides of the pastry with water.
   Gently place the strips onto the edges of the rectangle to make a flat frame. Lightly
   prick the bottom of the pastry and brush with apricot jam (jelly). Return the baking
   sheet to the fridge for 1 hour before baking. This stabilizes the dough and ensures
   that the butter is truly cold so the pastry will remain flaky.
4. For the filling, in a stand mixer or with a hand-held electric whisk, beat together
   the cream cheese or mascarpone with the icing (confectioners') sugar. Stir in the
   flour or cornflour (cornstarch) and citrus zest, and set aside.
5. Halve the apples or pears and remove the cores. Cut into pieces 4mm (¼in)
   thick. If you're using fresh figs, slice them into 5mm (¼in) rounds. Set aside.
6. Preheat the oven to 210°C fan (410°F/Gas 6).
7. Smear the cheese filling evenly over the tart. Avoid the sides so they can
   properly puff up while baking. Arrange the sliced fruit in a nice pattern on top
   of the filling. Beat the egg with the water. Lightly brush the frame with the egg
   glaze. Sprinkle the fruit with some Demerara (raw) sugar.
8. Bake in the preheated oven for 40–45 minutes. Check the tart after 30 minutes;
   if it is taking on too much colour, cover with parchment and continue to bake.
   After 10 minutes, remove the parchment for the final 5–10 minutes of baking.
   Bake until the tart is beautifully puffed up and rich, golden colour. Do bake the
   tart *long enough*. Serve with a dollop of crème fraîche, if you like.

INDIVIDUAL TARTES TATIN

These are the ultimate classic pastry in mini size, just a few perfect nibbles. These minis are perfect for someone who enjoys just a bite or two! Pictured page 180.

MAKES 6

½ x quantity Rough Puff Pastry (see page 174) or Quick Whole-wheat Rough Puff Pastry (see page 175)

3 apples
50g (3 tbsp plus 1 tsp) butter
120g (½ cup plus 1½ tbsp) caster (superfine) sugar

1. Preheat the oven to 210°C fan (410°F/Gas 6) and lightly butter a 6-hole muffin pan. Cut pieces of parchment, about 11cm (4¼in) square. Shape the pieces of parchment over the end of a glass with the same diameter as an individual muffin hole. Place each piece of parchment into the muffin pan.
2. Peel, core and quarter the apples. Cut each quarter in half.
3. Melt the butter in a heavy frying pan over medium heat. Add the sugar and stir with a wooden spoon. Increase the heat. After a few minutes the sugar will melt and turn amber in colour. Remove the pan from the heat.
4. Place the apple slices in a single layer into the pan with the caramel. It will be crowded – the slices shrink while cooking.
5. Return the pan to the heat and cook the apples over a high heat for 15 minutes. Occasionally spoon the caramel and apple juices over the apples while they cook.
6. While the apples are cooking, remove the rough puff from the fridge. On a lightly floured work surface, roll out to 5mm (¼in) thick. Cut out 6 circles, about 7cm (2¾in) in diameter. Slice four steam slits into each circle.
7. Place the circles back in the fridge and remove the frying pan with the apples from the heat. Using a tablespoon, place four slices of apple and a little caramel in each of the muffin pan holes.
8. When all the holes are filled, cover each one with a circle of pastry.
9. Bake in the preheated oven for 13–15 minutes, or until golden brown. Let cool for 5 minutes before you run a knife along the edge and tip the tartlets out.

Chill
The tartes tatin can be kept in the fridge, covered airtight, for up to 1 day.

Freeze
Simply freeze the entire muffin pan at the end of step 8. When frozen, wrap airtight and store in the freezer for up to 6 months.

Bake from frozen
Preheat the oven as above and bake for 14–16 minutes until golden brown.

CINNAMON TWISTS

I never get tired of cinnamon and sugar. Though I grew up simply sprinkling it on toast, I was later introduced to the joy of snickerdoodles. Then I discovered how a bit of cinnamon and sugar elevates whipped cream. When laminated in a flaky pastry, cinnamon and sugar will caramelize and morph into a completely new taste sensation: earthy, sweet and mellow. Pictured page 181.

MAKES 12

100g (½ cup) caster (superfine) sugar

½ x quantity Rough Puff Pastry (see page 174)

Filling

75g (6 tbsp) sugar (I like to use raw cane sugar, it caramelizes nicely)

2 tsp ground cinnamon

1 tsp ground turmeric (optional)

1. Combine the sugar and spice(s) for the filling and set aside.
2. Spread 3mm (⅛in) of caster (superfine) sugar on your work surface. No flour. Roll out the dough to a rectangle 20 x 30cm (8in x 12in) and sprinkle generously with the sugar and spice mixture. Fold the bottom end of the dough into the centre, then the other end over it, like a letter. Turn the dough so the closed edge is on the right.
3. Sprinkle more sugar on your work surface and repeat the laminating process by rolling out the dough to a rectangle 20 x 30cm (8in x 12in) and sprinkle generously with the sugar and spice mixture. Fold the bottom end of the dough into the centre, then the other end over it, like a letter. Turn the dough so the closed edge is on the right. Wrap the dough in parchment and refrigerate for 30 minutes to let the gluten relax and the butter chill.
4. Preheat the oven to 220°C fan (425°F/Gas 7). Brush a bit of water onto a baking sheet, then line with parchment. This creates steam while baking.
5. Roll out the chilled dough on a layer of plain sugar into a rectangle 30cm (12in) wide, 20cm (8in) deep. Trim the sides and edges so they are even.
6. Using a pizza wheel or a sharp knife, cut the dough into 2.5cm (1in) wide strips. Working quickly, twist each strip several times, then place on the prepared baking sheet, 4cm (1½in) apart.
7. Bake for 13 minutes, or until golden and the sugar is lightly caramelized. Let cool on the baking sheet for 10 minutes, then transfer to a rack to cool completely.

Chill

The laminated dough can be kept in the fridge, wrapped airtight, for up to 1 day.

Freeze

Open freeze the twists after step 5. When frozen, transfer to an airtight bag and store in the freezer for up to 6 months.

Bake from frozen

Preheat the oven as above and bake on a lined baking sheet for about 13 minutes, or until golden.

PISSALADIÈRE

Enjoy the south of France wherever you are with this fabulous pissaladière recipe!
Some people use pizza dough, but I love the puff pastry texture.

SERVES 8

3 tbsp olive oil

500g (1lb 2oz) onions,
  thinly sliced

2 garlic cloves, finely minced

1 tsp salt

1 bay leaf

several sprigs of thyme

½ x quantity Rough Puff
  Pastry (see page 174) or
  Quick Whole-wheat Rough
  Puff Pastry (see page 175)

16 anchovy fillets, drained

20 Niçoise olives

1. In a large frying pan, heat the olive oil over medium heat and add the onions, garlic, salt and herbs. Lower the heat and cover the pan for 5 minutes until the onions have given off some liquid. Remove the lid, raise the heat a bit and continue to sauté until the onions are wilted and transparent. This can take up to 20 minutes. Give it time. Transfer the onions to a bowl to cool thoroughly before using. (Don't put warm onions on the puff pastry or it will ruin the layers.)

2. When the onions have cooled, preheat the oven to 200°C fan (400°F/Gas 6). Brush a bit of water onto a baking sheet, then line with parchment. This creates steam while baking.

3. Roll out the dough to a 22 x 32cm (8½ x 12½in) rectangle and place on the parchment. If at any point you feel the dough sticking, put it back in the fridge to cool for 15 minutes before proceeding.

4. Using a ruler, even up the sides of the dough so all four sides are straight, then cut off 2cm (¾in) of dough from all sides. Lightly brush the edges of the tart with water and place the cut dough on top of the tart edges to form a frame.

5. Distribute the cooled onions evenly over the tart. Place the anchovies and olives on top of the onions. Bake in the preheated oven for 21–23 minutes until the pastry is lightly coloured and puffed up. Enjoy warm or at room temperature.

CHEESE STICKS

Never serve alcohol at a party without a bit of food. Well, here's your bit-of-food: cheese sticks. Have you ever wondered what garlic-herb-cheese perfume smells like? This is it.

MAKES 20

½ x quantity Rough Puff Pastry (see page 174) or Quick Whole-wheat Rough Puff Pastry (see page 175)

½ x quantity Garlic Herb Butter (see page 214), softened

50g (generous ½ cup) grated Parmesan cheese

1 egg, lightly beaten, to glaze

1. Taking the half portion of puff pastry, let's laminate the dough one last time with cheese and garlic butter. Roll out the dough to a rectangle, about 20cm (8in) long and 1cm (½in) thick. Spread half the garlic butter on the upper two-thirds of the rectangle, then sprinkle with one-third of the grated cheese. Fold the bottom end of the dough into the centre, then fold the other end over it, like a letter. You will have three layers of dough. Rotate the dough so the closed edge is on the right.

2. Roll out the dough again to 20cm (8in) long and 1cm thick (barely ½in) rectangle. Smear the rest of the garlic butter on the upper two-thirds of the dough. Sprinkle with half the remaining cheese. Fold the bottom third to the centre, fold the top third over it like a letter. Wrap in parchment and chill for at least 20 minutes. At this stage the dough can be kept in the fridge for up to 2 days.

3. When you're ready to bake, preheat the oven to 220°C fan (425°F/Gas 7). Brush a bit of water onto a baking sheet, then line with parchment. This creates steam while baking.

4. On a lightly floured surface, roll out the dough to a 15 x 40cm (6 x 16in) rectangle. Using a pizza wheel or knife, cut the dough into 2cm (¾in) wide strips.

5. Working quickly, twist each strip several times, then place on the prepared baking sheet, 4cm (1½in) apart. Brush each twist with the lightly beaten egg and sprinkle with the remaining cheese.

6. Bake in the preheated oven for 15 minutes until golden and the cheese is melted. Let cool on the baking sheet for 10 minutes before transferring to a rack to cool completely.

Chill
The folded dough can be kept in the fridge, wrapped airtight, for up to 2 days.

Freeze
Place the individual twists on a plate in the freezer. When frozen, transfer to an airtight bag and freeze for up to 6 months.

Bake from frozen
Preheat the oven as above and bake on a lined baking sheet for 15 minutes until golden.

FRESH TOMATO AND CHEESE TART WITH HERBS

Maybe you're planning a picnic. Even if it's simply on your living-room rug, this tart will give you that perfect laid-back feeling of eating anywhere but at your dining table. Use any kind of tomatoes you can get your hands on, even those not perfectly ripe will bake up into something delicious! Pictured opposite in a square shape.

SERVES 8

600g (1lb 5oz) cherry tomatoes, halved (or large tomatoes, cut into 1cm/½in slices)

2 garlic cloves, thinly sliced

½ teaspoon salt

plain (all-purpose) flour, for dusting

½ x quantity Rough Puff Pastry (see page 174) or Quick Whole-wheat Rough Puff Pastry (see page 175)

125g (1½ cups) finely grated cheese, such as Parmesan, Comté or an aged Cheddar

herbs, such as tarragon, lemon thyme and/or parsley, finely chopped

1 tbsp olive oil

1 egg, beaten

1. Preheat the oven to 200°C fan (400°F/Gas 6). Brush a bit of water onto a baking sheet, then line with parchment. This creates steam while baking.
2. In a large bowl, mix the tomatoes and garlic with the salt. Let stand for 10 minutes. Drain off the liquid and place the tomatoes in a single layer on paper towels to dry.
3. On a lightly floured work surface, roll out the dough to a 24 x 30cm (9½ x 12in) rectangle and place on the parchment. If at any point you feel the dough is getting sticky, put it back in the fridge to cool for 15 minutes before proceeding.
4. Using a ruler, even up the sides of the dough so all four sides are straight, then cut off 2cm (¾in) of dough from all sides. Lightly brush the edges of the tart with water and place the cut dough on top of the tart edges to form a frame.
5. Sprinkle the dough with half of the grated cheese and half of the herbs, followed by the tomatoes and garlic. Drizzle with the olive oil. Scatter the rest of the cheese on the tomatoes, save the rest of the herbs to use after baking. Brush the tart edge with beaten egg.
6. Bake in the preheated oven for about 35 minutes until the pastry is golden. Check the colour of the tart after 25 minutes; if it's taking on too much colour, cover with parchment. Remove from the oven and sprinkle with the rest of the fresh herbs. Let cool briefly before serving!

ELEGANT ONION TART WITH THREE CHEESES

I just happened to have three cheeses in my fridge for this recipe. If you only have two or would like to use four, be my guest. Like planning a seating chart for a dinner party, just make sure whatever cheeses you choose get along. Pictured page 187 in a round shape.

SERVES 8

30g (2 tbsp) butter

1 tbsp olive oil oil

400g (14oz) onions, thinly sliced

½ tsp salt (I love to use smoked oak salt)

2 tsp balsamic vinegar

75g (⅔ cup) crumbled blue cheese, such as St. Agur or Vermont's Bayley Hazen Blue

125g (generous ½ cup) ricotta cheese

35g (scant ½ cup) finely grated Parmesan cheese

½ x quantity Rough Puff Pastry (see page 174) or Quick Whole-wheat Rough Puff Pastry (see page 175)

50g (scant ½ cup) walnut halves, coarsely chopped (optional)

1 egg, beaten

1. In a large frying pan, heat the butter and oil over medium heat. Add the onions and salt. Lower the heat, cover the pan and cook for 5 minutes until the onions have given off some liquid. Remove the lid, raise the heat a bit and continue to sauté for 10 minutes. Add the vinegar and let bubble up until the vinegar is cooked down.

2. Transfer the onions to a bowl to cool completely before using. (Don't put warm onions on the puff pastry or it will melt the butter and ruin the flakiness.)

3. In a small bowl, use a fork to combine the blue cheese with the ricotta. Set aside.

4. When the onions have cooled, preheat the oven to 200°C fan (400°F/Gas 6). Brush a bit of water onto a baking sheet, then line with parchment. This creates steam while baking.

5. Roll out the dough to a 24 x 30cm (9½ x 12in) rectangle, and place on the parchment. If at any point you feel the dough is getting sticky, put it back in the fridge to cool for 15 minutes before proceeding.

6. Using a ruler, even up the sides of the dough so all four sides are straight. Then cut off 2cm (¾in) of dough from all sides. Lightly brush the edges of the tart with water and place the cut dough on top of the tart edges to form a frame.

7. Sprinkle a small amount of Parmesan cheese over the pastry, followed by an even layer of onions. Distribute spoonfuls of ricotta and blue cheese over the onions, and sprinkle the remaining Parmesan cheese and optional walnuts over the tart. Brush the edges with the egg.

8. Bake in the preheated oven for 22–24 minutes until the crust is lightly coloured and the cheese is golden. Enjoy warm or at room temperature.

CREAM CHEESE DOUGH

Cream cheese dough is so delicious! It is amazing as a 'lid' for pot pies, to use for turnovers and is also great for little hand pies. It is so light and flaky – a little effort goes a long way! This recipe makes enough for 10 turnovers, 12 hand pies, 12 'lids' for 10cm (4in) pot pies, or 1 Tarte Soleil (see page 190).

MAKES 600G (1LB 5OZ)

250g (1¾ cups) plain (all-purpose) flour, plus extra for dusting

¼ tsp salt

180g (1½ sticks) butter, cold and cut into small pieces

180g (¾ cup) cream cheese, cold

2 tbsp water, very cold

1. In a large bowl, combine the flour and salt.
2. Add the butter and cream cheese. Use your fingertips to break up the pieces of fat into small bits.
3. Add the cold water and, with a fork, mix to combine.
4. Turn the dough onto a lightly floured work surface and quickly shape the dough into a round disc.
5. Wrap in parchment and refrigerate for 2 hours before use. The dough can be kept in the fridge for up to 3 days.

Tip To make lids for deep dish or pot pies, on a lightly floured surface roll the dough to a thickness of 5mm (¼in) and cut into circles 5mm (¼in) wider than the diameter of the baking pan. Make 4 slits in each one to allow steam to escape during baking. Use immediately or freeze for up to 6 months.

Chill
The dough can be kept in the fridge wrapped airtight for up to 3 days.

Freeze
The dough can be kept in the freezer, wrapped airtight, for 6 months. You can also freeze individual portions. When frozen, transfer to an airtight bag and store in the freezer for up to 6 months.

Defrost
Let the dough thaw overnight (or for at least 5 hours) in the fridge. Let individual portions thaw for several hours in the fridge before using.

TARTE SOLEIL

My father could barely boil an egg, but, strangely, a tarte soleil was in his entertaining repertoire! The difference between his and mine is my cream cheese dough, of course.

SERVES 8

1 x quantity Cream Cheese Dough (see page 189)

450g (1lb) frozen spinach, thawed

3 tbsp finely chopped mixed herbs, such as tarragon, dill, parsley, and/or lemon thyme

1–2 spring onions (scallions), finely chopped

1–2 garlic cloves, finely chopped

75g (½ cup) crumbled feta cheese

finely grated zest of 1 lemon

salt and pepper

1 egg, for glazing

1. Make the cream cheese dough and refrigerate for at least 30 minutes. The colder the dough, the easier it is to work with.
2. Spread the thawed spinach on a kitchen towel, roll it up and wring it out very well to remove as much liquid as possible, otherwise the spinach will make the dough soggy!
3. Chop the spinach and mix with the herbs, spring onions (scallions), garlic, feta, lemon zest, and salt and pepper, and set aside.
4. Preheat the oven to 200°C fan (400°F/Gas 6). Prepare two sheets of parchment and place one on a baking sheet. Set aside. Lightly beat the egg.
5. Roll out half of the dough. Using a saucepan lid or a plate, cut out a circle approx. 30cm (12in) in diameter. Place the dough on the baking parchment and return it to the fridge. Roll out the remaining dough, cut out a circle to 30cm (12in) in diameter and place it on the baking sheet with the parchment.
6. Brush a 3cm (1¼in) border of the dough with some beaten egg. Spread the filling on top of the dough and leave 2cm (¾in) of border free. Place the chilled circle of dough on top of the filling. Press the edges of the dough together to seal.
7. Now take a glass approx. 5cm (2in) in diameter and place it in the centre of the circle. Using a knife, cut the circle into quarters, starting at the glass and working outwards. Cut each quarter into three pieces. Now simply twist each piece several times. Brush generously with egg glaze and sprinkle with salt and pepper.
8. Bake the tart in the preheated oven for 25–27 minutes until golden.

Tip: Other delicious fillings include Simple Garlic Butter (see page 214) and a handful of grated Parmesan cheese, or Simple Tomato Sauce (see page 215) with 75g (½ cup) crumbled feta cheese and some chopped fresh herbs.

CHERRY POCKET PIES

When my daughters were little, they shared a room and were ecstatic when we moved and everyone had their own space. Think of these pocket pies as your own space.

MAKES 12

1 x quantity Cream Cheese Dough (see page 189)

300g (10½oz) pitted cherries or blueberries, fresh or frozen and thawed, plus a bit of juice (not more than 3 tbsp), if using frozen berries

75g (6 tbsp) caster (granulated) sugar

1½ tbsp cornflour (cornstarch)

pinch of salt

water, to seal the edges of dough

1 egg, beaten with 1 tsp water, for brushing

For glazing (optional)

4–5 tbsp icing (confectioners') sugar

2 tsp milk, or more as needed

1. Make the cream cheese dough and refrigerate for at least 30 minutes. The colder the dough, the easier it is to work with.
2. Combine the cherries or blueberries, their juice, sugar, cornflour (cornstarch) and salt in a saucepan over a medium heat. Bring to a slow boil while constantly stirring. Boil for about 1 minute until the filling begins to thicken. Transfer to a bowl to cool completely before using. Do not put a hot filling on cold dough.
3. Preheat the oven to 200°C fan (400°F/Gas 6) and line a baking sheet with parchment.
4. When the dough is thoroughly chilled, cut it in half horizontally. Put half of dough back in the fridge while you roll out the other half to about 3mm (⅛in) thickness. Using a glass or a 12cm (4¾in) cookie cutter, cut out rounds.
5. Place up to 1 tablespoon of filling in the middle of the round. Brush the edges with water to seal. Either fold the dough over to make a half-moon pocket pie or place another piece of dough on top of the filling. Using the tines of a fork, seal the edges. Chill each pie as you go along until all pies are ready to bake.
6. Before baking, gently cut two or three slits into the surface of each pie and brush with the beaten egg and water to give the pie a nice finish. Bake in the preheated oven for 16–18 minutes, checking after 13 minutes for colour and covering loosely with a piece of parchment, if necessary.
7. Combine the glaze ingredients, if using, until a good dripping consistency is achieved. Drip the glaze onto the pocket pies, and serve!

CROSTATA DOUGH

A crostata has a kind of rustic quality that I simply love. I like to add a bit of polenta (cornmeal) to the dough for a bit of golden colour and that extra bite. Together with some lemon zest, this crostata – whether you make it sweet or savoury – is like a little sunshine on your plate.

**MAKES 550G
(1LB 3OZ)**

200g (1¾ sticks) butter, chilled

225g (1⅔ cups) plain (all-purpose) flour, plus extra for dusting

50g (⅓ cup) coarse polenta (cornmeal) (do not use instant polenta)

1 tsp caster (granulated) sugar

grated zest of 1 lemon

¾ tsp salt

80ml (⅓ cup) water, very cold

1. Cut the butter into thin slices and put in the fridge. Combine the flour, polenta (cornmeal), sugar, lemon zest and salt into a big bowl.
2. Add the butter to the flour mixture. Use your fingertips to work the butter into the flour until it resembles large peas. Add the cold water. Using a fork, barely mix to combine.
3. Turn the dough onto a lightly floured work surface, lightly knead it, and quickly shape it into a disc, about 15cm (6in) in diameter. The secret to a light and flaky crust is not just cold butter and water, but also not handling the dough too much.
4. Wrap the dough in parchment and refrigerate for at least 30 minutes. The dough needs to be well chilled before it can be rolled out.

Chill
The dough can be kept in the fridge, wrapped airtight, for up to 3 days.

Freeze
The dough can be kept in the freezer, wrapped airtight, for up to 6 months.

Defrost
Let the dough thaw overnight (or for at least 4 hours) in the fridge.

CHEESE AND TOMATO CROSTATA

This is the perfect alternative to pizza or quiche, is oh-so-delicious and GREAT for a picnic, too! You can use just about anything in your fridge.

SERVES 8

1 x quantity Crostata Dough (see page 194)

Garlic Chilli Oil, to taste (see page 216)

50g (⅔ cup) grated Parmesan cheese

handful of Slow-roasted Tomatoes (see page 216)

4–5 tbsp ricotta cheese

1 egg, beaten, to glaze (optional)

1. Chill the crostata dough for at least 30 minutes prior to baking.
2. Preheat the oven to 210°C fan (410°F/Gas 6) and line a baking sheet with parchment. Roll out the dough on a lightly floured work surface until it is about 5mm (¼in) thick. Cut out a 35cm (14in) circle and place on the baking sheet.
3. Smear the dough with garlic chilli oil. Sprinkle with half the grated Parmesan cheese and spoon the tomatoes into the centre of the dough, leaving a 5cm (2in) border. Spoon the ricotta cheese on top of the filling and sprinkle the remaining grated Parmesan on top of the ricotta. Lift up the edge of the dough and pinch to form a vertical seam. Continue around the crostata, pinching a seam every 6cm (2½in) to form a standing border. Fold the border down over the edge of the filling. Brush the folded border with egg glaze.
4. Bake in the preheated oven until the crust and filling are golden, 25–30 minutes. Check after 18 minutes and cover with parchment if it's taking on too much colour. Slide the crostata onto a rack to cool.

Spiced corn filling variation Sauté a chopped onion in 2 tbsp olive oil and a pinch of ground cumin until translucent. Add 1–2 diced tomatoes and 100g (⅔ cup) frozen corn. Continue to cook until the mixture is thick and cooked through. Sprinkle 25g (⅓ cup) grated Parmesan cheese onto the dough, followed by the vegetable mixture, 4–5 tbsp ricotta cheese and another 25g (⅓ cup) grated Parmesan cheese.

Mediterranean veg filling variation Preheat the oven to 210°C fan (410°F/Gas 6). Put 1 sliced red (bell) pepper, 1 sliced yellow (bell) pepper, 1 thinly sliced onion and 1 sliced courgette (zucchini) or aubergine (eggplant) on a baking sheet. Pour over 2 tbsp olive oil and sprinkle on some salt. Roast for 20–25 minutes. Let cool, then drain the vegetables of any roasting liquid. Sprinkle 25g (⅓ cup) grated Parmesan cheese onto the dough, followed by the vegetable mixture, 125g (½ cup) ricotta, some freshly chopped herbs, toasted pine nuts and another 25g (⅓ cup) grated Parmesan cheese. Pictured page 195.

MIXED FRUIT CROSTATA

This is the Italian version of an American free-form pie and very quick to throw together. I love, LOVE the polenta (cornmeal) in the crust. It gives it such a beautiful colour and slightly crunchy texture. Pictured page 195.

SERVES 8

1 x quantity Crostata Dough (see page 194)

50g (¼ cup) caster (granulated) sugar

15g (2 tbsp) plain (all-purpose) flour

pinch of salt

about 750g (1½lb) up to 3 kinds of fresh, seasonal fruit, such as raspberries, blackberries and sliced pineapple, apples, pears and nectarines

some freshly grated ginger, to taste (optional)

1 egg, beaten

1 x quantity Sweet Nut Streusel (see page 211, optional)

1. Chill the crostata dough for at least 30 minutes prior to baking.
2. In a medium bowl, stir together the sugar, flour and salt. Mix in the fruit and ginger, if using, and let stand until the fruit juices are released, gently stirring occasionally, about 15 minutes. Make sure not to break up the berries, if using, when you stir the fruit.
3. Preheat the oven to 210°C fan (410°F/Gas 6) and line a baking sheet with parchment.
4. On a lightly floured work surface, roll out the crostata dough to about 5mm (¼in) thick. Cut out a 35cm (14in) circle. I like to use the large lid of a pan for this! Transfer the dough to the baking sheet.
5. Spoon the fruit (and some of the juices) into the centre of the dough, leaving a 5cm (2in) border all around. Lift up the border of dough and pinch to form a vertical seam. Continue around the tart, pinching a seam every 6cm (2½in) to form a standing border. Fold the border down over the edge of the fruit. Brush the border with egg glaze and sprinkle streusel over the fruit, if desired.
6. Bake in the preheated oven until the crust is golden and the fruit filling is bubbling at the edges, about 25–30 minutes. Check for colour after 18 minutes and cover with parchment if the crostata is taking on too much colour. Slide the crostata onto a rack to cool. Serve warm or at room temperature with ice cream or whipped cream.

EXIT

RAS

EXTRAS

I love to 'get dressed up' and I love accessories: earrings, scarves, rings – you name it. But as my husband always says, look in the mirror before leaving the house and remove one item. He's right! The same goes for *baking accessories*: frostings, buttercreams, streusels and fillings. Enjoy them and be judicial in their use. Less is often more – allow each element to shine. Use fillings and frostings to complement a pastry, to highlight flavour and texture, rather than overpower it.

LESS IS OFTEN MORE – ALLOW EACH ELEMENT TO SHINE

TIME TO GET DRESSED UP

Streusels, both sweet and savoury, are one of my favourite secret weapons in the kitchen. The Florentine Cake-ie (see page 61) simply comes alive with that extra, cheesy crunch on top! And who knew that cornflakes would add so much flavour and texture in a streusel?

My selection of frostings, buttercreams and fillings encompasses the whole range, from super quick frostings to a fancy Swiss meringue buttercream, and from rich buttery toppings to indulgent vegan options.

Your choice of recipe often depends upon the time you have to invest in making it. Have no fear, even the quickest frostings are stellar. I especially love the classic ermine frosting, which I have updated to include a vegan version – simply delicious! And if you've never tried a tahini frosting or a salted caramel made with miso, here's your chance. Feel free to follow my suggestions for combining these accessories with certain pastries or follow your own vision and taste. Trust yourself, experiment, be bold and remember, less is often more.

Brilliant buttercream

When making a Swiss meringue buttercream, the temperature of the butter is critical: if it's too soft, the buttercream will be runny. Just whip in some cooler butter in small amounts to correct. If the butter is too cold, the buttercream will curdle. Simply whip in some very soft butter in small amounts to compensate. Do make sure the meringue is sufficiently cooled before adding the butter.

When making any kind of icing (confectioners') sugar-based frosting, make sure the butter is soft, though cream cheese should be cool. You must use either a hand-held electric whisk or a stand mixer, and whip, whip, whip at high speed for many minutes to create a fluffy, airy frosting. If you want to add melted chocolate, always stir it in by hand followed by some sifted cocoa to intensify the flavour (a small amount of instant coffee or espresso powder will also intensify the chocolate flavour – simply dissolve a spoonful in a tiny bit of hot water and beat in with the icing (confectioners') sugar).

Give it up for ganache

A simple ganache can be one of your strongest allies in the kitchen. Leave it warm for a velvety chocolate sauce or let it cool and thicken for a rich filling or frosting. Add some raspberry purée or grated orange zest for a subtle, fruity tang.

VANILLA

Vanilla is one of my essential ingredients. I use it to add flavour to all sorts.

VANILLA SALT

Vanilla salt is perfect in almost every sweet recipe. Here is how to make it!

MAKES 150G (5OZ)

VEGAN

GLUTEN-FREE

150g (¾ cup) coarse sea salt
2–4 vanilla pods (beans)

1. Finely grind the salt with the vanilla pods (beans) using a spice grinder or a pestle and mortar.
2. Stored in a jar, vanilla salt simply gets better with time and keeps forever.

VANILLA EXTRACT WITH ALCOHOL

I travel with a small bottle of vanilla extract – that's how perfect it is!

MAKES 200ML (¾ CUP PLUS 1½ TBSP)

VEGAN

GLUTEN-FREE

2–3 vanilla pods (beans)
200ml (¾ cup plus 1½ tbsp) vodka or any other kind of 40% spirit (rum is also good)

1. Cut the vanilla pods (beans) in half lengthways and put directly into a sterilized jar or bottle. Do not scrape out the seeds! Add the alcohol to cover.
2. Shake twice a week. Let steep for a couple of weeks before using.

VANILLA EXTRACT WITH GLYCERIN

This vanilla extract without alcohol has a slightly sweet flavour.

MAKES 300–500ML (1¼–2 CUPS)

GLUTEN-FREE

3–4 vanilla pods (beans)
300–500ml (1¼–2 cups) glycerin

1. Cut the vanilla pods (beans) in half lengthways and put directly into a sterilized jar or bottle. Do not scrape out the seeds! Add enough glycerin to cover.
2. Shake several times a week. Let it steep for 1–2 months before using.

MISO CARAMEL WITH SEA SALT

Miso is made from fermented soya beans (soybeans) and grains (usually rice or barley) mixed with salt and a fungus called *Aspergillus oryzae* (koji in Japanese). Many people know miso as a soup... and now as salted caramel.

MAKES 250ML (1 CUP)

VEGAN OPTION

GLUTEN-FREE

150g (¾ cup) caster (superfine) sugar

70ml (scant ⅓ cup) water

150ml (½ cup plus 2 tbsp) cream (or use coconut milk for plant-based)

1 tbsp light miso

1 tsp vanilla extract (see page 202)

several pinches of sea salt

1. Thoroughly clean a medium-sized pot with a lid, add the sugar and water and bring to the boil over medium heat. Cover with a lid and let boil for 3 minutes. Do not stir: the sugar crystals can settle on the walls of the pot and crystallize the caramel.

2. Remove the lid and let everything simmer gently for about 8 minutes until the sugar has dissolved and the colour is golden.

3. Once the mixture is slightly browned, remove from heat and whisk in the cream or coconut milk. The moment the liquid is added, the mass bubbles up and can even seize up and get lumpy – but have no fear! Add the miso, vanilla extract and several pinches of sea salt. Now let the caramel simmer for about 5 minutes so all the ingredients can amalgamate and thicken. The longer you cook the caramel, the thicker it gets! Allow the sauce to cool before use.

4. When the caramel has cooled, simply put in a sterilized jar and cover. Store in the fridge for up to 4 weeks.

Use as
- a flavour to frostings or buttercreams
- a drip on cakes
- a filling in the Parsnip Miso Cinnamon Swirl Bread (see page 152) – make sure the caramel is pretty thick when used as a filling
- an ice cream topping

CLASSIC ERMINE FROSTING

I love ermine frosting! Use it in warm weather when you want the added stability of a buttercream without eggs. Dress it up with various add-ins or keep it elegant and simple. This is also a great buttercream for piping.

**MAKES 700G
(1LB 8OZ)**

GLUTEN-FREE

150g (¾ cup) caster (superfine) or Demerara (raw) sugar
pinch of salt

1 tsp vanilla extract (see page 202)
250ml (1 cup) milk

40g (⅓ cup) cornflour (cornstarch), sifted (see note)
250g (2 sticks) butter, softened

1. Put the sugar, salt, vanilla extract and milk in a small pan and, stirring constantly, heat slowly until the sugar has dissolved.
2. Whisk the cornflour (cornstarch) into the hot milk mixture over medium heat. Continue to stir while the mixture thickens; this will take a few minutes.
3. As soon as the mixture is thick like a pudding, remove from the heat and transfer to a bowl to cool. If the mixture seems lumpy, first put through a fine sieve (strainer) before transferring it to a bowl.
4. Place cling film (plastic wrap) directly onto the surface to prevent a skin from forming. Let cool for about 20 minutes before placing in the fridge to chill.
5. Using a stand mixer or hand-held electric whisk, beat the butter until creamy. Gradually add the cooled 'pudding' and continue whipping vigorously until the frosting is light and airy.

Note Cornflour (cornstarch) makes the frosting very velvety and the 'pudding' may not need to be sieved (strained). You can also use flour in a pinch.

Additions You could add several tablespoons of Miso Caramel with Sea Salt (see page 203), your favourite jam (jelly) or lemon curd. For a chocolate version, heat 100g (3½oz) chopped plain (semi-sweet) chocolate with the milk until it melts. Whisk in 3 tbsp sifted unsweetened cocoa powder and proceed with step 2. For a mocha version, whisk instant espresso into the hot milk.

Chill
Refrigerate in an airtight container for up to 10 days. To use, gently warm it to room temperature over a water bath or in the microwave and beat until fluffy.

Freeze
Store in the freezer for up to 1 year.

Defrost
Let thaw in the fridge overnight or on your kitchen counter. When thawed, whip up again to a spreading consistency.

VEGAN ERMINE FROSTING

This is a fabulous, velvety frosting that you can use as a frosting for cake-ies and snacking cakes or as a filling for tiered cakes.

MAKES 700G (1LB 8OZ)

VEGAN

GLUTEN-FREE

150g (¾ cup) caster (superfine) or Demerara (raw) sugar

pinch of salt

1 tsp vanilla extract (see page 202)

250ml (1 cup) unsweetened plant-based milk

40g (⅓ cup) cornflour (cornstarch), sifted (see note, page 200)

250g (9oz) margarine, softened

1. Put the sugar, salt, vanilla extract and plant-based milk in a small pan and, stirring constantly, heat slowly until the sugar has dissolved.
2. Whisk the cornflour (cornstarch) into the hot milk mixture over medium heat. Continue to stir while the mixture thickens; this will take a few minutes.
3. As soon as the mixture is thick like a pudding, remove from heat and transfer to a bowl to cool. If the mixture seems lumpy, first put through a fine sieve (strainer) before transferring it to a bowl.
4. Place cling film (plastic wrap) directly onto the surface to prevent a skin from forming. Let cool for about 20 minutes before placing in the fridge to chill.
5. Using a stand mixer or hand-held electric whisk, beat the margarine until creamy. Gradually add the cooled 'pudding' and continue whipping vigorously until the frosting is light and airy.

Additions You could add several tablespoons of plant-based Miso Caramel with Sea Salt (see page 203), your favourite jam (jelly), or a drop or two of gel food colouring. For a chocolate version, heat 100g (3½oz) chopped vegan plain (semi-sweet) chocolate with the plant-based milk until it melts. Whisk in 3 tbsp sifted unsweetened cocoa powder and proceed with step 2. For a mocha version, whisk instant espresso into the hot milk.

Chill
Refrigerate in an airtight container for up to 10 days. To use, gently warm it to room temperature over a water bath or in the microwave and beat until fluffy.

Freeze
Store in the freezer for up to 1 year.

Defrost
Let thaw in the fridge overnight or on your kitchen counter. When thawed, whip up again to a spreading consistency.

CREAM CHEESE FROSTING

As Aristotle said, 'the whole is greater than the sum of its parts,' which can also be said for this frosting. The key to its perfection is really whipping it up. Whip it longer than you think, at a higher speed than you deem necessary. You will be rewarded.

MAKES 475G (1LB 1OZ)

GLUTEN-FREE

175g (¾ cup) cream cheese

100g (6½ tbsp) butter, softened

200g (1⅔ cups) icing (confectioners') sugar, sifted

1. Using a stand mixer or hand-held electric whisk, whip together the cream cheese and the butter.
2. Add the icing (confectioners') sugar and whip on high speed for several minutes until light and fluffy.

Why not try adding
- a few tablespoons of strawberry jam (jelly)
- a tablespoon of finely ground freeze-dried berries, or more to taste
- a few tablespoons of Miso Caramel with Sea Salt (see page 203)
- a few tablespoons of lemon curd
- up to 3 tablespoons maple syrup or honey
- some lemon, lime or orange zest

Chill
Refrigerate in an airtight container for up to 10 days. Bring to room temperature then whip until creamy.

Freeze
Freeze in an airtight container for up to 6 months.

Defrost
Let thaw, then whip until creamy and soft.

CHOCOLATE FROSTING

This is the simplest of chocolate frostings, yet simple can also be simply delicious!

MAKES 450G (1LB)

VEGAN OPTION

GLUTEN-FREE

150g (5oz) plain (semi-sweet) chocolate (use vegan chocolate for plant-based)

150g (1¼ sticks) butter, softened (or use 150g/⅔ cup margarine, softened, for plant-based)

150g (1¼ cups) icing (confectioners') sugar, sifted

1 tbsp unsweetened cocoa powder, sifted

1. Melt the chocolate and set it aside to cool.
2. With a stand mixer or hand-held electric whisk, beat the butter or margarine until creamy. Add the icing (confectioners') sugar and beat on high speed for several minutes until fluffy. Switch to a spatula and gently but thoroughly mix in the melted chocolate, followed by the cocoa (don't beat in the chocolate).

Chill
Refrigerate in an airtight container for 10 days. Bring to room temperature, then stir until spreadable.

Freeze
Freeze in an airtight container for up to 6 months.

Defrost
Let thaw, then stir until spreadable (do not whip).

TAHINI FROSTING

Tahini is one of those surprise ingredients for me, delicious in sweet or savoury dishes.

MAKES 525G (1LB 2½OZ)

VEGAN OPTION

GLUTEN-FREE

150g (1¼ sticks) butter (or use 150g/⅔ cup margarine for plant-based)

175g (¾ cup) tahini

200g (1⅔ cups) icing (confectioners') sugar, sifted

1 tsp vanilla extract (see page 202)

1 tsp instant espresso powder, dissolved in 1 tsp hot water

pinch of salt

1. With a stand mixer or hand-held electric whisk, beat the butter or margarine until creamy. Add the tahini and icing (confectioners') sugar.
2. Beat for several minutes until fluffy. Whip in the vanilla extract, espresso and salt.

Chill
Refrigerate in an airtight container for 1 week. Bring to room temperature, then whip until creamy.

Freeze
Freeze in an airtight container for up to 6 months.

Defrost
Let thaw, then whip until creamy and soft.

CLASSIC GANACHE

Ganache is simply a catch-all name for chocolate melted with cream. It can be a sauce, a dip, a filling or a frosting. Ganache thickens when it cools, so if you want a sauce, use it immediately, but if you want to use it as a filling or frosting, let it cool and thicken to a spreading consistency.

**MAKES 600G
(1LB 5OZ)**

300g (10½oz) plain (semi-sweet) chocolate, finely chopped

300ml (1¼ cups) double (heavy) cream

1. Place the chocolate in a big bowl. Heat the cream to boiling point and pour over the chocolate. Cover without stirring for 5 minutes.
2. Uncover and stir with a whisk until the chocolate is completely melted and the mixture is smooth. Cool to room temperature. Refrigerate until a thick spreading consistency; about 2 hours.

Variations

- for orange ganache, add the zest of 1 orange and 1 tbsp Cointreau to the cream before boiling
- for fruity ganache, use 200ml (¾ cup plus 1½ tbsp) cream and add 100ml (scant ½ cup) fresh and sieved (strained) raspberry, blackcurrant or redcurrant purée

Chill

Refrigerate in an airtight container for up to 7 days. Gently warm and beat well to a spreadable consistency.

Freeze

Freeze in an airtight container for up to 3 months.

Defrost

Thaw in the fridge overnight. Warm to slightly soften and beat well to a spreadable consistency.

CLASSIC GERMAN BUTTERCREAM

German buttercream is custard-based, very creamy and light in texture and easy to make. If you'd like to augment the flavour, you could try the additions on page 206. And remember, like any buttercream, the butter needs to be just the right temperature – not too cold, but not too soft! If it does curdle because the butter was too cold, warm the buttercream (only for a few seconds) then beat vigorously until it comes together and is light and airy. If the buttercream is too soft because the butter was too warm, then simply beat in a few teaspoons of cool butter until the buttercream has a spreadable consistency.

**MAKES 600G
(1LB 5OZ)**

GLUTEN-FREE

200ml (¾ cup plus 1½ tbsp) whole milk

1 tsp vanilla extract (see page 202)

100g (scant ½ cup) caster (superfine) sugar

1 tbsp cornflour (cornstarch)

pinch of salt

3 egg yolks

200g (1¾ sticks) butter, softened

1. In a medium saucepan, heat the milk and vanilla extract until almost boiling.
2. In a small bowl, combine the sugar, cornflour (cornstarch) and salt. Whisk in the egg yolks and continue to beat until light and creamy.
3. Whisk half of the warmed milk into the egg yolk mixture, then add this mixture to the rest of the milk in the saucepan. Allow the mixture to thicken over medium heat, stirring constantly with a spatula so that it does not burn; it'll take a few minutes. As soon as the mixture has thickened like a 'pudding', remove from the heat.
4. Transfer to a bowl and place cling film (plastic wrap) directly on the surface to prevent a skin from forming.
5. Place the bowl on a rack to cool for about 20 minutes. Then set in the fridge to cool completely, at least 45 minutes.
6. With a stand mixer or hand-held electric whisk, beat the softened butter until creamy. Gradually add the cooled 'pudding', bit by bit. Continue to whip vigorously until the buttercream is light and airy.

Chill
Refrigerate in an airtight container for up to 4 days. Carefully warm in a microwave or over a double boiler until slightly soft, then beat well to a light and spreadable consistency.

Freeze
Store in the freezer for up to 3 months.

Defrost
Let thaw in the fridge overnight. When thawed, carefully warm in a microwave or over a double boiler until slightly soft, then beat well to a light and airy, spreadable consistency.

SWISS MERINGUE BUTTERCREAM

Dearest baker/pastry lover, if you have never made Swiss meringue buttercream, now's your chance! There are a few utensils you absolutely need: a thermometer; a heatproof bowl that can sit inside a pan of water; and a hand-held electric whisk or stand mixer.

**MAKES 550G
(1LB 3OZ)**

GLUTEN-FREE

½ tsp any light vinegar

¼ tsp salt

200ml (¾ cup plus 1½ tbsp) egg whites (about 5–6 egg whites)

160g (¾ cup plus 1 tbsp) caster (superfine) sugar, Demerara (raw) sugar or brown sugar

200–280g (1¾–2½ sticks) butter, softened, to taste

Optional extras

2 tsp vanilla extract (see page 202)

up to 150ml (½ cup plus 2 tbsp) fresh raspberry or strawberry purée

150ml (½ cup plus 2 tbsp) lemon curd

200g (7oz) plain (semi-sweet) chocolate, melted

1 tbsp instant espresso powder mixed into 1 tsp boiling water

almond extract, to taste

1. Wipe the vinegar and salt around a large mixing bowl, a whisk and the beaters of an electric hand-held whisk or the whisk attachment and bowl of a stand mixer. Do not rinse. This stabilizes the egg whites and makes sure everything is grease-free.
2. Combine the egg whites and sugar in the clean mixing bowl and set it over a pan of simmering water. Make sure the base of the bowl doesn't touch the water. Using a hand whisk, beat the eggs and sugar until frothy. Whisk intermittently while the mixture warms. In about 3–4 minutes, the mixture will read 72°C (162°F). This is the temperature at which salmonella bacteria are killed.
3. When the egg whites and sugar reach 72°C (162°F), remove the bowl from the hot water and continue to beat this mixture in your stand mixer or with an electric hand-held whisk. Remember, the bowl is HOT. Set the bowl on top of a towel so it doesn't rotate while you beat. Beat at high speed for a few minutes until the mixture thickens. In about 6–8 minutes, the meringue will have stiff peaks. Continue to beat until the mixture is no longer warm.
4. Make sure that butter is soft and the meringue is cool to the touch. Lower the mixer speed to medium and add the butter, a tablespoonful at a time.
5. After all butter is incorporated, other flavours or food colouring can be added.

Chill

Refrigerate in an airtight container for up to 10 days. Bring to room temperature and beat to a fluffy, spreadable consistency before use.

Freeze

Freeze in an airtight container for 6 months.

Defrost

Thaw overnight in the fridge. Bring to room temperature and beat to a fluffy, spreadable consistency before use.

STREUSEL TOPPINGS

I have always been a big fan of streusel, and not only since living in Germany! These versions are great on cake-ies – mix and match, as you please. I could also imagine making one of the pizzas (see pages 126 and 140) as a fruit pizza topped off with one of the sweet streusels… or even use your fave granola instead of the cornflakes.

SAVOURY STREUSEL

MAKES 200G (7OZ)

100g (3½oz/3 slices) wholemeal (whole-wheat) or white sliced bread

80g (1 cup) coarsely grated cheese (I like to use a combination of Parmesan and Gruyère)

3 tbsp olive oil

Put the bread in a food processor and process to make breadcrumbs. Combine with the grated cheese. Stir in the olive oil to coat evenly. Transfer to an airtight container and refrigerate for up to 1 month or freeze for up to 6 months.

SWEET NUT STREUSEL

MAKES 375G (13OZ)

100g (generous ⅔ cup) pecan or walnut halves, chopped

50g (⅓ cup) plain (all-purpose) flour

100g (½ cup) caster (granulated) sugar

1½ tsp ground cinnamon

pinch of salt

125g (1 stick) butter, cold and cut into thin slices

Combine the nuts, flour, sugar, cinnamon and salt. Using your fingertips, work in the cold butter to form a coarse streusel. Transfer to an airtight container and refrigerate for up to 1 month or freeze for up to 6 months.

CORNFLAKE STREUSEL

MAKES 135G (4¾OZ)

70g (scant 1½ cups) cornflakes, lightly crushed

20g (2 tbsp) Demerara (raw), brown or white sugar

pinch of salt

45g (3 tbsp) butter, softened

Mix the lightly crushed cornflakes, sugar and salt. Work in the softened butter to make a loose streusel. Transfer to an airtight container and refrigerate for up to 1 month or freeze for up to 6 months.

HOMEMADE GRANOLA

Making granola yourself is so rewarding. It also has the added benefit that it perfumes your kitchen with the most wonderful, nutty, maple-y scents.

**MAKES 500G
(1LB 2OZ)**

VEGAN

150g (1½ cups) oats
(I like a mix of coarse/
steel-cut and fine oatmeal
or rolled/old-fashioned
oats)

100g (generous ¾ cup)
walnut or pecan halves,
coarsely broken

50g (⅔ cup) desiccated
(dried unsweetened
shredded) coconut

1 tbsp linseeds (flaxseeds)

¼ tsp salt

¼ tsp ground cinnamon

3 tbsp maple syrup

3 tbsp vegetable oil

30g (2 tbsp) light or dark soft
brown or muscovado sugar

150g (1 cup) mixed dried
fruit, such as raisins,
cherries, cranberries or
finely chopped dates

1. Preheat the oven to 150°C fan (300°F/Gas 2) and line a baking sheet with parchment.

2. Combine the oats, nuts, coconut, linseeds (flaxseeds), salt and cinnamon in a bowl. Set aside.

3. In a small pan whisk together maple syrup, oil and sugar. Heat until the sugar is dissolved. Fold into the oat mixture, making sure to coat everything thoroughly.

4. Spread the mixture evenly over the baking sheet and bake in the preheated oven for 25 minutes until lightly toasted.

5. Remove from the oven and transfer to a large bowl. Immediately stir in the dried fruit. Let cool completely, then store in an airtight jar for up to 6 months.

BUTTERS

Each of these butters is like a magic kitchen wand. Spread as a filling, the savoury butters infuse a bread with a subtle, warm flavour. Used as a spread, they punch a wallop! And just about everything tastes better with honey butter.

HONEY BUTTER

MAKES 150G (5OZ)

GLUTEN-FREE

100g (6½ tbsp) butter, softened

50g (3 tbsp) runny honey

pinch of salt

pinch of ground cinnamon

pinch of ground turmeric

For the honey butter, whip the butter and honey with the salt and spices until light and fluffy.

GARLIC HERB BUTTER

MAKES 80G (3OZ)

GLUTEN-FREE

1–2 garlic cloves

½ tsp sea salt

75g (5 tbsp) butter, softened

handful of herbs, finely chopped, such as chives, tarragon, lemon thyme, marjoram, etc

For the garlic butter, crush and finely mince the garlic with the salt, then combine with the butter and chopped, fresh herbs.

CHEESY GARLIC HERB BUTTER

MAKES 100G (3½OZ)

GLUTEN-FREE

3 garlic cloves (trust me)

¾ tsp sea salt

30g (2 tbsp) butter, softened

1 tbsp olive oil

3 tbsp brewer's yeast or finely grated cheese

a few scrapings of lemon zest

1 small chilli, finely chopped

handful of finely chopped herbs, such as chives, sage, tarragon, thyme or parsley

Crush and mince the garlic cloves with the sea salt. Combine with the butter, olive oil, brewer's yeast or cheese, lemon zest, chilli and herbs.

SIMPLE TOMATO SAUCE

Lots of people have a go-to tomato sauce, hopefully not out of a jar. This is mine: quick and straightforward. Depending upon my *vision*, I like to dress it up with various spices or herbs. Use your imagination, be creative, and maybe… just maybe… this recipe will become your new kitchen bestie.

MAKES ENOUGH FOR 3 PIZZAS

VEGAN

GLUTEN-FREE

2 garlic cloves
¾ tsp sea salt
3 tbsp olive oil
2 x 400g (14oz) cans of Italian peeled plum tomatoes
pinch of sugar

Optional extras
crushed chilli
crushed fennel seeds
your favourite herbs

1. Crush and mince the garlic cloves with the sea salt.
2. Heat the olive oil in a large pot over medium heat. Add the garlic and sauté for about 2 minutes. The sea salt brings out the flavour of the garlic, keeps the garlic moist and prevents it from over-browning. If you are adding crushed chilli or fennel seeds, add them now.
3. Squish the plum tomatoes (I like to do this by hand). Add them, along with their juice, to the garlic. Slowly bring the tomato sauce to a boil, add the sugar and reduce the heat. Simmer for about 30–45 minutes, depending on how thick you want the sauce to be. If you are adding fresh herbs, do so right before serving for the most vibrant flavour.

Tip The sauce can be further reduced to use as a dip for the Cheese Sticks (see page 185); as a filling for Seedy Filled Flatbreads (see page 143); or as a topping for Sourdough Flatbreads (see page 129).

Chill
Keep the sauce covered in the fridge for up to 5 days.

Freeze
When completely cooled, freeze the sauce in an airtight container for up to 6 months.

Defrost
Thaw in the fridge overnight.

SLOW-ROASTED TOMATOES

These tomatoes are the simplest of simple, the most delicious gift that keeps on giving. Why? Because you can literally use any old tomatoes, they don't even need to be particularly ripe. And in less than 90 minutes, you have something beautiful. Elevated.

MAKES 500G (1LB 2OZ)

VEGAN

GLUTEN-FREE

500g (1lb 2oz) cherry tomatoes, halved

3–4 tbsp your favourite olive oil

salt

dried chilli flakes (hot red pepper flakes), to taste (optional)

a few sprigs of rosemary or thyme (optional)

1. Preheat the oven to 150°C fan (300°F/Gas 2) and line a baking sheet with parchment.
2. Place the tomatoes in a large bowl and combine with the olive oil.
3. Place the tomato halves, cut-side up, onto the prepared baking sheet. Sprinkle with salt and dried chilli flakes (hot red pepper flakes), if using. Add a few sprigs of rosemary or thyme, if you have them.
4. Bake in the preheated oven for 1 hour 10 minutes–1 hour 20 minutes until the tomatoes have taken on a nice colour and are caramelized.
5. Remove from the oven and discard any herbs. Let cool on the baking sheet. With the help of the parchment, gently transfer the tomatoes to a bowl. Store, covered airtight, for 2 weeks in the fridge.

GARLIC CHILLI OIL

If you ever feel like you need to spice up your life, look no further. Great as a bread dip, it is perfect to spread onto a crostata or flatbread before layering on the veggies.

MAKES 250ML (1 CUP)

VEGAN

GLUTEN-FREE

250ml (1 cup) oil (either a fruity olive oil or more neutral vegetable oil)

4 whole, dried red chillies

2 garlic cloves, peeled and left whole

½ tsp whole peppercorns, black or mixed colours

½ tsp dried chilli flakes (hot red pepper flakes)

1. Combine all the ingredients in a small saucepan over low heat and cook gently for 20 minutes to infuse the oil. Do not let the garlic take on any colour.
2. Remove the pan from the heat and let the mixture cool.
3. When cool, transfer to an airtight sterilized jar. Store for up to 1 year.

INDEX

THANK YOU

It takes a village, and this book is no exception! First and foremost, I'd like to thank my family for their patience, expert taste-testing skills and willingness to sample yet another version of sourdough buns. A huge thanks also goes to my team – the best in the world for keeping Barcomi's alive in my absence. I am so grateful for Steph Milner, Lucy Philpott, Bess Daly and Amy Cox at DK UK, as well as Monika Schlitzer at DK Germany for their support and input. It has been a pleasure working with Kate Reeves-Brown, whose detailed editing has made every word count! And lastly, this book would be nowhere without the commitment, talent, and high standards of Lisa Linder, Max Faber and Elif Ergin. What a lucky person I am! Thank you all.

Publisher Acknowledgments

DK would like to thank Gillian Haslam for proofreading, Hilary Bird for indexing and Susan Stuck for recipe testing.

DK LONDON

Editors Kate Reeves-Brown, Lucy Philpott
Designers Hannah Naughton, Amy Cox
Senior Acquisitions Editor Stephanie Milner
Design Managers Bess Daly, Marianne Markham
Senior Production Editor Tony Phipps
Senior Production Controller Stephanie McConnell
Jacket Designers Hannah Naughton, Amy Cox
Jacket Coordinator Jasmin Lennie
Art Director Maxine Pedliham
Publishing Director Katie Cowan

Photographer Lisa Linder
Prop Stylist Elif Ergin
Food Stylist Max Faber

First published in Great Britain in 2022 by
Dorling Kindersley Limited
DK, One Embassy Gardens, 8 Viaduct Gardens,
London, SW11 7BW

The authorised representative in the EEA is
Dorling Kindersley Verlag GmbH. Arnulfstr. 124,
80636 Munich, Germany

Copyright © 2022 Dorling Kindersley Limited
A Penguin Random House Company
10 9 8 7 6 5 4 3 2 1
001–328207–Aug/2022

A CIP catalogue record for this book
is available from the British Library.
ISBN: 978-0-2415-5315-2

Printed and bound in China

For the curious
www.dk.com

ABOUT THE AUTHOR

Born in Seattle and educated in New York, Cynthia Barcomi arrived in Berlin in the mid 80s to pursue her career as a professional dancer. Cynthia had her first child in 1988 and decided: 'it's time to roast coffee beans and bake cheesecake!' What followed were two cult restaurants and eight German-language baking books. Cynthia makes regular appearances on German television as 'The Berlin Baking Queen' and teaches online baking classes to thousands of followers.

Cynthia is married to the American film actor Harvey Friedman and has four children, two cats and eight chickens.

Find more at cynthiabarcomi.com, her online shop, her newsletter and the Cynthia Barcomi app.